HELP YOURSELF
FOR TEENS

HELP YOURSELF FOR TEENS

Real-Life Advice for Real-Life Challenges

DAVE PELZER

A PLUME BOOK

PLUME
Published by Penguin Group
Penguin Group (USA) Inc., 375 Hudson Street, New York, New York 10014, U.S.A.
Penguin Group (Canada), 90 Eglinton Avenue East, Suite 700, Toronto, Ontario,
Canada M4P 2Y3 (a division of Pearson Penguin Canada Inc.)
Penguin Books Ltd., 80 Strand, London WC2R 0RL, England
Penguin Ireland, 25 St. Stephen's Green, Dublin 2, Ireland
(a division of Penguin Books Ltd.)
Penguin Group (Australia), 250 Camberwell Road, Camberwell, Victoria 3124,
Australia (a division of Pearson Australia Group Pty. Ltd.)
Penguin Books India Pvt. Ltd., 11 Community Centre, Panchsheel Park,
New Delhi – 110 017, India
Penguin Books (NZ), cnr Airborne and Rosedale Roads, Albany, Auckland 1310,
New Zealand (a division of Pearson New Zealand Ltd.)
Penguin Books (South Africa) (Pty.) Ltd., 24 Sturdee Avenue, Rosebank,
Johannesburg 2196, South Africa

Penguin Books Ltd., Registered Offices: 80 Strand, London WC2R 0RL, England

First published by Plume, a member of Penguin Group (USA) Inc.

First Printing, September 2005
10 9 8 7 6 5 4 3 2 1

Ⓟ REGISTERED TRADEMARK—MARCA REGISTRADA

LIBRARY OF CONGRESS CATALOGING-IN-PUBLICATION DATA

Pelzer, David J.
    Help yourself for teens : real-life advice for real-life challenges / David Pelzer.
        p.   cm.
    ISBN 0-452-28652-2
    1. Teenagers—Conduct of life.   2. Adolescent psychology.   3. Interpersonal
relations in adolescence.   4. Resilience (Personality trait)   5. Abused teenagers—
Psychology.   I. Title.
    HQ796.P394 2005
    158'.0835—dc22

                                                                2005007484

Printed in the United States of America
Set in Garamond Light

DEDICATION

Without reservation the prominent dedication of this book is to my son, Stephen. A caring young man with your whole life ahead of you. It is my hope, my dream, and my single passion for you to apply all that you have learned for the greater good and achieve your greatness. Stephen, to me you are nothing short of a gift from God.

To anybody and everybody who works with young adults: teachers, juvenile counselors, staff members, social workers, judges, advocates, foster care organizations, law enforcement officials, to the endless agencies in America and throughout the world, on behalf of serving, protecting, and rescuing those in peril, I thank you.

This book is also dedicated to you, the reader. With every word of every page, I pray with all my heart that it makes a connection. That it enables one to stop, think, and appreciate life with all its chaos and wonders for what it truly is—a grand adventure. For more than a decade you the reader have allowed me into your life and for many into your hearts. I am forever grateful.

And finally, for the sole purpose of bestowing honor, it is my privilege to pay homage to those who wear the uniform: the proud, the brave, the selfless individuals of America's armed forces. For those of you in harm's way: Execute your duties faithfully, be safe, and come back in one piece. The world is watching and praying for you all. You've always had and will continue to have my deepest respect. Godspeed!

CONTENTS

THE DEAL

I want you to succeed. From this moment on, with every day that passes, with everything you strive for, I wish, I *want* for you to achieve your greatness. That's it. Period. If you get nothing else from this book—if you decide to throw it away or feed it to the shredder—I've made my point. At this stage in your life, striving to better yourself is imperative.

Now, when I say *succeed,* I'm not referring to the wasteful, gluttonous, shallow, ego-driven lifestyle of the bored, rich, and shameless. But, hey, if you've worked hard, sacrificed, and earned enough dough to buy a four-hundred-foot limo with a waterfall in the back spilling into a bubbling Jacuzzi, if that's what you truly want, I say *go for it*. What I am referring to is that guttural, never-yielding determination that you can tap into and apply at will. And no matter what you've been through or are currently dealing with, you can prevail—*and* prevail with a sense of dignity and honor.

I'm adamant for a reason. I know firsthand how brutal life can be. For more than eight years, starting before I was in preschool and lasting through the fifth grade, my mother—a hateful, psychologically sick alcoholic—

subjected me to constant physical and mental torture. She nearly killed me several times. One time Mother accidentally stabbed me, and since she refused to take me to the hospital for fear of exposure, the wound became so infected that days later in the basement, where I lived, I practically crawled over to a water basin and cleaned the yellowish pus-filled wound myself. When Mother refused to feed me for fourteen days, I snuck water from the same water basin; but before doing so I thought ahead, making certain my worn shoes wouldn't squeak or the water pipe wouldn't vibrate when I opened the tap—which would give me away. When my mother forced me to stay in a bathroom with a deadly combination of ammonia and bleach—which can asphyxiate a person in a matter of minutes by filling up the lungs with thick mucus—all I had to do was immediately stay low to the floor, throw a rag into the toilet bowl, and wrap it around my mouth and nose while praying the left-side vent would pump in fresh air.

I was in no way heroic or courageous. In all instances thinking in terms of black and white, I adapted. All I had to do was rely on myself and think ahead. I didn't do anything extraordinary. Like millions of folks faced with a situation, when push came to shove, I simply did whatever I had to do.

When I was twelve, my teachers and other school staff called the authorities. Had it not been for these saviors, who at that time risked so much for me, there is not a doubt in my mind that my disturbed mother would have killed me. Years later I discovered that my case was considered one of the worst child-abuse cases that year in California's history. I was incredibly lucky.

Once removed from my mother, I was placed in foster care as a ward of the court until I reached the legal age of adulthood. It was during my teen years that my long, long road to recovery began. As much as I naively imagined, I couldn't simply flip a switch and shut off all I had been subjected to. If anything, that's when my troubles began. I quickly discovered that surviving my mother was minor in comparison to adjusting to the real world. My well-planned defensive mechanisms that kept me alive in the past suddenly became absolute hindrances. My magician-like sleight-of-hand techniques I had developed for staying alive all those years made it easy for me now in foster care to gleefully steal candy, clothes, and anything I could get my sticky hands on—not only for my own selfish greed, but also to give my bounty to others who would *allow* me to be their friends. Because of my sheer desperation to be accepted, I practically did and said anything and acted in ways that were nowhere close to who I really was. I was fully aware I was wrong, and I knew that I easily allowed myself to be used, but after years of living in a basement— isolated from my family, who by my mother's orders weren't permitted to even look at me, let alone speak my name—the need for me to belong was too intense. Since Mother did not permit me to speak in her house, I had been stifled for so long that now by reflex I often lashed out in the most colorful of nouns whenever threatened. To make matters worse, whenever I became nervous, which was the majority of the time, I stuttered uncontrol- lably. I felt that the more I tried to fit in, be cool, or act tough, the more I sunk deeper in societal quicksand.

As my inner frustration grew, my attitude became cold and dark. For years school had been my protective solace, but now it became an institution that wasted *my* time, forcing me to learn something that wouldn't amount to anything in my adult life. I refused to turn in homework, I daydreamed in class, and I acted like a fool. In a matter of months I transformed into a pint-sized incorrigible ass. To this day I have no idea how or why so many genuinely and kindly guiding foster parents, social workers, teachers, consolers, and everyday folks put up with me. But my reign of self-absorbed destruction came to an end when I was fourteen and was booked in juvenile hall as a high-strung delinquent and repetitive runaway, under suspicion of arson. Partly because of my cocky "I don't give a damn" and "No one's gonna tell me what to do" attitude, my ruse nearly backfired when in a brief evaluation a county psychiatrist practically boasted to my social worker in front of me that due to my pent-up frustration and being socially isolated, and after years of intense physical and emotional abuse, that I was most likely destined to repeat the vicious cycle of hate and despair. And if I stayed on my present course, by the time I reached eighteen I would end up dead or, more likely, in prison.

If that wasn't enough, as I sat and pondered my fate in juvenile hall, beginning to realize the repercussions of my actions, my foster parents discovered to their horror that my mother, informed of my behavior, desperately fought to convince the county that it was in *their* best interest to have me committed to a mental facility.

In life, especially as a teenager, I believe there is a selected number of wake-up calls. For me, one of those occasions was absorbing the words *reach eighteen . . . death . . . prison . . . mental institution*.

After surviving all that I had, I refused to allow myself

to become swallowed by my past. What brought me back from the brink of self-destruction were people in my face every day giving me commonsense advice, expecting and at times demanding the absolute best from me. And part of it was luck, for if I did a fraction of what I did in today's world, I would have been locked up for good.

It's amazing what a reality check, positive determination, a little luck, and a small amount of time can do for a person's outcome. But it's not always easy. As I was dealing with my past, struggling to stay on the straight and narrow, I still had to work through everyday realities of life as well. As a foster kid in junior high, and because the county had a very limited clothing allowance, I found myself scorned simply because I didn't have the latest, coolest clothes that seemingly everyone else wore. Determined to do something, I spent some of the money I earned from shining shoes or as a busboy at a local restaurant to buy the exact clothes I wanted. And because I lacked basic motor skill development, much to my public embarrassment I couldn't center the ball for the school team during football games no matter how hard I tried. I was responsible for more errors in one play than anyone in the school's history. I couldn't catch the easiest of pop fly balls in baseball or hit a ball with a bat or shoot a basket. But there was one thing I could do: RUN. For years my mother had me run to and from home and school at strict precise times; otherwise I'd receive a twisted form of punishment. I wasn't the fastest kid on the track team, but at least I could do something halfway decent, which was a tremendous boost for my esteem. Yet *talking*—formulating plain everyday words in front of others—was the one thing I absolutely dreaded. Much of the time my mother refused to let me speak in her house, and being forced to swallow tablespoons of ammonia that burned my tongue and esophagus, I became nervous at school and would stutter . . . especially when I was confronted by the school bullies, which happened every—and I mean *every*—single day. I stuttered uncontrollably to the point that I'd become so frustrated, I would burst into tears for all to see. Yet back at my foster home within the refuge of my bedroom, I'd close the door for privacy, stand in front of the mirror, and slowly pronounce each letter of the alphabet, studying my lips and then closing my eyes while listening to the exact sound coming out. Initially I was consumed with frustration, but after some time and after studying different characters in the action movies I liked to watch, I began to communicate well enough that I would imitate an entire scene from a movie.

Again, for me it certainly wasn't easy or immediate. In high school the social pressure seemed enormous. I never did "fit in." I never got to hang out, and I never went out. If anything, I was the class spaz. Because of a reputation that followed me everywhere, I couldn't do anything that was acceptable in front of my peers. And it hurt deeply. Developing so late in adolescence and not knowing the basics about hygiene, I had so many pimples on my chin, I was dubbed crater face. Back then, if you looked up in the dictionary the words *geek, spaz, nerd, dork, doofus,* and *idiot,* you would most likely have seen a photo of me with volcanic blotches, coke-bottle glasses with thick black frames, long, straggly, matted hair, and off-colored chipped teeth smiling back.

In all my years I learned a number of things. One of them is that when it comes to social standing or outward appearances, today's overly awkward ugly duckling can be tomorrow's radiant swan or a warty toad can transform into a handsome prince.

Again, it's remarkable what time, some perseverance, and a little luck can do to turn everything around. Nearly twenty years to the month after I was rescued, I went from one of the worst cases of child abuse in California to one of the country's Ten Outstanding Young Americans. Other recipients include Presidents Kennedy, Nixon, and Clinton and internationally acclaimed individuals, entertainers, and sports celebrities. All of these individuals are known for their efforts in assisting others, including my childhood heroes Chuck Yeager and Christopher Reeve. A year later I flew to Kobe, Japan, to humbly be the only American recipient of The Outstanding Young Person of the World. As a young teen who couldn't handle the pressure and constantly fumbled a football, a short time later in the U.S. Air Force I not only became a paratrooper but a certified Combat Air Crew Member responsible for the precise and delicate task of midair refueling of the top-secret air force jets. Then one day years later, not looking for anyone, a beautiful redhead came into my life, became my best friend, and years later my lovely bride. As of this writing I am a father to a teenager, a young man who is gracious, grounded, and one of the kindest souls I've ever known. I have been self-employed for many years. I encourage others to better themselves through my seminars, books, and, more important, by example. I still do a great number of comic impersonations, but now I do so onstage. I love to make folks laugh and feel good about themselves, and I love to be optimistic, respectful, and appreciative about life and the greatness of America. I am healthy, completely free of the chains from my past. I am living life to the fullest. Above all, rain or shine, rich or poor, good times or bad, **I am happy.** Think of it: What more can I or anyone else truly ask for?

Please understand, I am not exposing my childhood for reasons of extracting sympathy in any way, shape, or form. There are millions of folks who have been put through so much more than I. And I am in no way trying to flaunt whatever recognition or successes I have been fortunate enough to receive. Speaking frankly, I don't deserve them. I never set out to do anything for reasons of fame or fortune, and I never dreamt that I would somehow be blessed with all the opportunities that came my way. I am showing you through vivid *real* examples that no matter where you come from, no matter how absolutely dark or disheartening things are, may have been, or may become, if you can at the very least survive, then you can and should take positive control, turn things around, and achieve your own greatness! *Now* do you understand the maxim? **I want you to succeed!**

For more than twenty years I have had the privilege of working with young adults. From juvenile hall, jail, and foster care to more than seven thousand school assemblies, you name it, I've done it. Over time I've learned more from young adults directly than any seminar or any classroom curriculum combined. Notice that I did not mention the word *children*. I do not work with children. I do not play the guitar as I sing, *I love you, you love me, everybody take a pee.* I'm not here to fill your head with *Yummy Yum Sugarplum Stories* or *1,001 Poultry Broth for the Spirit Tales.* Why? I'm not here to waste your time. As a teen you're busy enough as it is and going in a zillion different directions. As you read these words, your body and your mind are developing and absorbing thousands upon thousands of physical and psychological changes. *Now,* add to that equation everyday life *and* whatever baggage you may be carrying. My job is to help you better yourself. My responsibility as your author is to help you identify problems before forming bad habits and to provide realistic solutions to them. I'm here to push you beyond your comfort zone, to help you, along with a host of others in your life, into adulthood. That's my job. No smoke, no mirrors, no cuddly little teddy bear–like creatures that bounce up and down chirping out sounds that make absolutely no sense to me.

I know what works. Although I do not have a degree in psychology, I've studied a great deal and continue to absorb as much as I can to have the most pertinent information. And after traveling to every state in this great nation of ours as well as to countries all over the globe and learning from different cultures, the single constant that shines above all is that nothing can conquer or dominate the human spirit. Absolutely nothing. No matter the odds or how defeating things may seem, we all have a chance of achieving greatness. And no matter what new-age philosophies that seemingly sprout up every other month with a new super-duper quick-fix concept that will seemingly solve all your problems with the snap of a finger or whatever enchanting weekend retreat you may attend, the truth is that these marvelous ideas wither before they can take root. Times change, but fundamental concepts stand head and shoulders above all. In other words, the basics work. Day in, day out, year in and year out, living an everyday lifestyle focusing on being productive and responsible while overcoming the trials of life, which have been handed down from generation to generation, has and always will prevail—especially when the philosophy-worshiping, reality-shirking gurus are off to something else. No matter your past, if you're alive and kickin', you still have a chance. **That's what works.**

With that stated, this book is broken down into three fundamentally separate yet interconnecting parts. All are crucial. The first section addresses problems you may be facing now or ones that may still be lingering from your past. The second section identifies the importance of decisions you make now and where they can lead you in your future. The third and final section points out that no matter how bad things get for you, never, absolutely never, give up on yourself.

As your author, my obligation is to provide you with the best information possible, without any gobbledygook, while being as direct and concise as possible. If a segment seems long, you can be assured that it's for your benefit. And at times I may seem overly stern. Please, never take me for being callous; however, I'm not here to be your bosom buddy. Think of me more as some quasi uncle or that hard-nosed coach who says things that aren't normally addressed and pushes you to achieve more than you think you're capable of achieving. But never forget with each word you read how much I and a host of others care deeply about your outcome. Why? For years I've seen firsthand thousands upon thousands of folks who, for whatever reason or excuse, stupidly throw away their hopes and ambitions, and end up wasting their lives. Consciously or subconsciously, the majority of these folks made those decisions at your age.

Your job is to pay close attention, absorb, *and* implement any and all parts of this book into your life. I highly recommend that if something jumps out at you while reading a section, you immediately highlight the area, dog-ear the page, or, better yet, jot down the excerpt on a three-by-five index card or sticky note so you can keep it with you whenever you feel the need for reassurance or inspiration.

Understand that this book is not going to identify or solve *all* your problems. With all my heart I truly wish it could, but that's not the reality of life and, more important, I have no intention of lying to you. However, together you and I will make one helluva dent.

The bottom line: Your life's outcome is solely up to you. If you can get out of bed in the morning, go to the bathroom, get dressed, and nuke something in the micro without any help, then **you** are capable of doing, achieving, and handling just about anything life can throw at you. You can do this. You can live up to your potential. And at your age, frankly speaking, I expect you to.

So here's the deal: I do my job and you do yours, and together we will do our best to advance you to your greatness. So, from this moment on, with every sentence of every paragraph of every section of every chapter, never, never forget how much I want, I pray, and I fight for your success.

—*Dave Pelzer*

Part One

DEALING WITH LIFE

Chapter 1

When Every Day Can Change Your Life

All of us know how important life is. But do you *really appreciate* how precious and how fragile life is and how it can be lost in a flicker?

Imagine, if you will, *you're* a middle-aged adult. Since the third grade you have dedicated every moment of every day of your life sacrificing to fulfill a dream: a one-in-a-gazillion chance of becoming an astronaut. Maybe the bug bit you when you were on the top bunk of your bed that you used as a spaceship, where you yelled out to your sister below, "Hey, let's go to the moon!" Or it might have been one of those carefree innocent moments that only the smallest of children seem to have, and even though you were viewed as an aggressive tomboy, when you lay down in your backyard on a clear summer's night, you fantasized about one day affording a telescope so you could be that much closer to the stars.

Time passes, and you jump through so many hurdles and overcome so much that it all becomes a blur. A short time ago you where an Eagle Scout or captain of the cross-country team. You may even have made a living as an acrobat or riding a seven-foot unicycle in the circus. Or maybe as a young person you never even gave NASA a thought but wanted to become a pediatrician instead—until it finally hit you what you truly wanted to become. You may have been turned down two, maybe three times, with nothing more than a form letter thanking you for applying but **". . . at this time we regret to inform you that you do not meet current mission requirements."** In other words: *Tough luck. Too bad. See ya.* But you're the kind of person that no matter the setback, you still push ahead. You never take no for an answer. You never quit. When push comes to shove, you blast through all obstacles.

One day you finally make it. You're on the team. *Now* the work begins—that is, after already obtaining a degree in aerospace engineering, astrophysics, or medicine, or the years of experience flying more than forty jets in the military. You're matched with a crew—a crew that becomes as close to you as a second family. You spend years together absorbing everything about your mission. You take a no-frills eleven-day "hike" in the high desert; you log thousands upon thousands of hours in flight/space simulators until you can predict the other person's move before he thinks it. All this, over five years, for a mere chance of a sixteen-day mission.

Then the big day comes. You couldn't sleep the night before the launch, and your heart is racing so fast that the NASA flight surgeon is concerned but knows all too well you're as giddy as a child on Christmas morning. You don your custom-fit orange "Pumpkin suit." You shake hands and exchange embraces with those from team NASA who will be with you in spirit every second of your journey. A swirl of emotions nearly overtakes you as you take the short walk to your RV-like transport that will drive you to the launchpad. Near you, thousands of cameras flash, all trying to capture that moment that will be etched in history: Seven souls again go where few have gone and fewer dare. There are more paparazzi than at the Oscars. You're bigger than Tom Cruise, Julia Roberts, Madonna, the New York Yankees, and the Super Bowl champions combined. You look for a glimpse of someone you know, someone you love, someone who is so proud of you that he or she can burst with pride, but the throng of onlookers makes it impossible. As you make your way, you carry more than the prescribed required equipment. You may have "smuggled" a few extra photos of your family. Maybe a lock of hair from your daughter or a fifty-nine-year-old tattered drawing of Earth as seen from the moon, sketched by a teenage boy who died in a Nazi concentration camp during World War II, the same camp that your mother and grandmother survived. You hear faint cries of *"God bless you." "Come home safely."* But by the time you soak it all in, you're strapped into your seat so tight that you can hardly breathe. During takeoff the g-forces are so intense, you feel as if some bear were sitting on top of you.

You reach orbit. You're free of gravity. For a few minutes you *are* that giddy kid at Christmas, that superhero who flies at ease, but for the next fifteen days you have work to do. You're so busy with your duties and experiments—ranging from the properties of fire in the absence of gravity, the transfer of genes in plants, how bones somehow lose their calcium properties, to studying weather patterns and observing how ants react in space—that your heart almost comes to a stop when you see in perfect clarity that small, dark blue-green marble spinning above your head. You hear such words as *"Spectacular,"* *"How insignificant and humble the sight it is,"* or the event is so powerful that mere words can hardly express it. Then beside you a crew member testifies, *"The quiet that envelopes space makes the beauty even more powerful, and I only hope that the quiet can one day spread to my country."*

In the midst of your mission one morning, your crew gathers for a rare time together. For a single minute of silence the seven of you pay tribute at the exact moment the space shuttle *Challenger* and its valiant crew were lost due to an explosion a mere seventy-three seconds after takeoff seventeen years ago.

Now, more than two weeks later and after millions of miles logged, you're again strapped in, this time for that ride home. The retro-rockets fire to slow down your shuttle even though you're still traveling at more than five miles a second. You reenter Earth's upper atmosphere, and a violent buckling begins as your craft glides back to Cape Canaveral. You can feel your space shuttle sway from side to side as the swooping wide S turns are used to further slow down your craft. You are now literally sixteen minutes from touchdown on your sixteen-day mission that seemingly began a lifetime ago . . . when something happens. A mechanical failure, a piece of debris from space, some unexplained anomaly? You may see a bright flash, maybe hear something that breaks loose. Hopefully you have enough time for a quick prayer.

Like everyone, when I heard the news that contact had been *lost* with the space shuttle *Columbia* and its crew, I didn't understand or appreciate the magnitude of the message. I simply hoped for the best. And like so many, I couldn't believe that after all the crew had endured before joining NASA and all they had accomplished as professional astronauts, that they could be *lost* so suddenly. The perfect quote that comes to mind is from President Bush: "The same creator who names the stars knows the names of the seven souls we mourn today."

Personally, I'm in such awe of those who make the impossible seem so natural. Again, we learn that space travel, while common, like life itself is still anything but commonplace.

Life *Does* Affect You

There may be a few folks who boast, "That will never happen to me. I'd never put myself at such risk." Well, no one's forcing you. For you and I now live in a time that the only word to describe the period is *bizarre*. Think that life can't be altered in a single moment or a single event? Read these numerals: **9/11.**

Now, picture in your mind where you were when you first heard the news. What were you wearing? Who were you with? What were you doing or about to do? What day-to-day problems were you facing that were so important, so overwhelming? And yet they suddenly vanished into thin air. There are few people who won't have that moment embedded in their psyche with perfect clarity forever: a beautiful late-summer day that changed the course of history and rallied a country against anarchy of the worst kind.

Like most folks, myself included, you may have been in absolute shock. No matter what you heard or saw as the events unfolded, you just couldn't believe it. Did you find yourself stating, "It must have been an accident!"? Or "It was like something out of the movies. It can't be real"? Then when reality took hold, it came on so suddenly that you couldn't breathe. You burst into tears. You held anyone that you could. You prayed, you cried, and you prayed some more. You may have felt an overwhelming dread as never before. "Could it happen here? Could it happen to me?" You called someone, then everyone. In the panic of chaos, nothing seems to matter but go home, stay home, and be with those you love.

As you read these words while that day is again revisited, ask yourself, and I do mean inquire *out loud,* without hesitation, "What really matters? What do **I** hold above anything of value?"

The answer: **Life.** To live, to breathe. To love and be loved. To watch that sunset while holding someone's hand, while listening to the background sounds of the ocean's waves crash upon the shore, and when that person casually turns, you not only capture a fragrance of their hair but can almost taste it. A moment so precious and yet so common that you hold it in your heart forever.

Life. To play, to discover any and all things. To do what you want, where you want, as you want. The opportunity to live in a country where life, liberty, and the quest for good times that never end is the national pastime. Music, television, CDs, portable CD players with batteries that never go dead. Friends, good times, bad times, crazy times. Lots and lots of laughs. You giggle, chuckle, and snort so much for no apparent reason that milk shoots out your nose, making you laugh all the more. First kiss, first date, first base, prom date. Tingly sensations, sweat, and fear rolled into one. Theme parks, concerts, fast food, and so much "movie butter popcorn" you can feel it seep from the bag and onto your pants, but you don't care. For your eyes are as wide as silver dollars locked onto the screen. Movies. Once a week, three times a week. Wide-screen, IMAX, 3-D. Action films, drama, "chick flicks," and more action films.

Life!

Piece of advice? Don't let life pass you by. Don't grow old too fast, and don't become consumed with situations that really don't amount to anything. It's not worth your energy and certainly not worth your time. If I may quote another line, this time from one of my favorite movies, *Hook,* when Robin Williams's character learns not to become so engrossed with all the pity problems that adults seem to become mired in while life passes them by: A loved one asks, "Have you lived out your last great adventure?" Robin's character places his hands on his hips as if he will forever be Peter Pan, the boy who refuses to grow old, and boldly smiles before stating, "To **live.** Now **that** would be an adventure!"

Please, all I'm saying—pleading, if you will—is for you to be mature enough and respectful enough to value the sanctify of life.

Now go out there and do something!

Help Yourself Reminders

- NEVER FORGET OR TAKE FOR GRANTED HOW PRECIOUS LIFE CAN BE AND HOW IT CAN ALL CHANGE IN A SINGLE MOMENT OR SINGLE EVENT.

- ALWAYS KEEP IN MIND WHAT IS TRULY IMPORTANT TO YOU.

Chapter 2

Hiding Behind Yourself

Care to know a secret? The single most important element that stops folks from reaching their full potential, from achieving greatness, **and** that robs them of the happiness they deserve is . . . **unresolved issues.**

Issues brushed aside. Problems left to fester and spread like cancer in our souls, that eat away at us day, after day, after day. All day, every day, because for whatever reason (or excuse), we didn't have the strength or courage to stand up for ourselves and confront and deal with these situations head-on and walk away a better, stronger individual.

In other words, folks who didn't *fully* deal with *and* get rid of their problems. And study after study proves again and again that these folks "developed," per se, this habit of either being totally oblivious, of procrastinating in situations, of burying their heads in the sand, or of clinging to their past predicaments at the "developmental age" in their lives: their preteen and teenage years.

Now, as a young adult, have you noticed that the older you become, the more problems seem to find you? And these predicaments, no matter how many you've already dealt with, only seem to escalate in number and in magnitude? And as you solve one problem, another—a far more outrageous situation—instantly takes its place?

How can this be? The straight answer: *It's life*. And there is not too much you or anyone else can do to escape it. Everybody, and I mean every single person on this planet, has problems. Rich kids, poor kids. The good-looking ones and the not so good-looking ones. Those who play sports, those in the school band, those in the drama department. Those who are extremely popular and seem to do no wrong, those who are stoic, tough-acting loners who always seem to be on the outside fringe.

And there are some situations that are totally out of your control. Parents, once madly in love, end up divorced. Loved ones who are the sweetest, kindest people in the world suddenly become ill and pass away. Someone you may have cared for deeply, whom you may have thought you'd be with forever, broke your heart. Maybe there was some dark, revolting past or, as previously illustrated, some unspeakable atrocity that occurred without warning or provocation.

Please understand, I am in no way trying to be disrespectful, nor do I intend to instantly discount someone's anguish. Absolutely not. All of us endure and deal with hurtful situations in different ways. And while there is no pain-o-meter, realize that what may not seem so overwhelming to you or your friends could be absolutely catastrophic to someone else.

And there are celebrities who, like you, have suffered in their teen years. Look at Tom Cruise, a very private, big-name action movie star who revealed in a rare interview moment about his parents' divorce. "I was eleven or twelve years old, and it was very, very painful for me. It was a summer I will never forget. But I also felt it was the right thing. I felt it was absolutely correct. My mother ended up raising us. I have a tremendous amount of admiration for her. Especially now, because I'm a father. And now I realize how hard she worked."

On top of all that, a young Mr. Cruise moved quite often, attending fifteen different schools. Yet with all the challenges around him, Tom used it to his advantage. "When you're traveling around . . . you see different cultures and how other people live. It really helped to form who I am. As an actor you play different characters. When I was in Kentucky, I wanted to pick up that Southern accent. When I was in Canada, I had that Canadian accent. And eventually you realize that when school is out, that is the world."

Now on the other side of a divorce is Al, an old friend of mine from foster care when I attended junior high. A few months into his parents' divorce, I could clearly see the definite changes occurring within one of the happiest, most outgoing people I've ever known. At first, like many kids his age who were confused, Al became cold, distant, and at times extremely volatile. One moment he was content, then suddenly he would become so incensed, I thought for sure he'd snap my head off. Over a short span of time, as much as I and some of Al's other friends tried to get him to open up, he became more defensive and withdrawn.

Back then in the midseventies the word *divorce* was new to teens our age, yet it suddenly seemed like some epidemic—parents were splitting up all over the place. I personally knew how hard it was for my dear friend since my parents had separated before I was taken away from my mother. Of all the things I faced during that time, my parents' separation was the worst. That cold, rainy wintry Saturday, after Mother gave Father his worldly belongings, she sped off, leaving one of San Francisco's bravest firemen standing alone in the chilling rain.

I also knew how confused Al felt to the point of becoming delusional, believing that if he had done "such and such," maybe things wouldn't have turned out so bad, or if he now did "so and so," his parents maybe, just maybe, would get back together. But a lot of us who truly knew Al and his folks realized it was a fantasy. By the time Al understood the cold, hard facts of life, he went off the deep end. Al stayed away from school for weeks at a time, ran away to everywhere and nowhere for no apparent reason, and fell into the disenchanting group of kids who also decided to drop out of life.

Mainly because I was transferred back and forth to different foster homes throughout the county, I bumped into my old friend years later at metal shop in high school. At first I didn't even know who he was. Al's face was weathered and beet red. His hair looked sweaty and was in unkempt layers. His clothes were torn and soiled, and he smelled as if he hadn't bathed in years. But the thing that shocked me the most was his eyes: They were dilated, bloodshot, and empty. He looked liked a walking zombie. When he tried to respond to something I said, Al, once known for his quick comedic wit, now lost his train of thought after a few seconds, making him unable to even say hello. The last time I saw my friend was when an ambulance rushed him from school after he fell to the floor screaming in pain after almost severing his hand with the metal grinder. After that, no one heard from Al again.

If I could wave a magic wand to erase whatever happened to you or anybody you know, I would most certainly do it in a heartbeat. But the reality of life is that you're not a preschool toddler who still believes in the tooth fairy; you are, in fact, a young adult on the cusp of your final stage of independence. Again, my job and that of others around you is to prepare you for dealing with any and all aspects of life. And this area is not only pivotal but critical. If you can't deal with problems effectively at this stage in your life (as intense as they may seem at this time), how are you going to live the next sixty-plus years? That's twenty-four **thousand,** four hundred and fifty-five days—all day, every day. Pretty miserably, I'd imagine. And that's no way to live.

Stuck in Their Mire

I cannot begin to tell you how many hundreds of thousand of adults I've met in their thirties, forties, and beyond who, for whatever reason(s), basically wasted their lives as a result of "something" that happened to them so many, many years ago. Again, a lot of folks who have become unfulfilled and unhappy, who made excuses, blamed others, or are filled with hatred, began their "journey of despair" at your age. I think that in itself is sad. Look at the math: Let's say there's a person in their fifties who—again, for whatever their reason or excuse—is still upset or even obsessed about something they experienced in their late teens. That's more than thirty years! Think of it: thirty years of anxiety and whatever needless suffering that went with it. What is more pathetic in this example is that this person wasted more time being upset, more than half their life, than the number of years when the problem first occurred (late teen years). And I'll bet that same type of person only adds unresolved problems on top of unresolved problems on top of . . . Are *you* getting the picture?

What truly breaks my heart are the dozens of young adults I came to know when I worked part-time in juvenile hall *and* the thousands of extreme hard-core cases I've worked with in other places who somehow, *through their own actions,* ended up in these facilities. How could this have happened? In part it happened because, yep, you guessed it, they did not deal with unfortunate situations the proper way and did not ensure that the vicious cycle didn't repeat itself—against themselves; they also amplified their pain to others.

Let's dispel a fable right now: **Do not believe** any nonsense that the enormous problem you may be facing right now, or how hard your upbringing may have been, that it **will** have an overwhelming **negative** impact on your adult life. That's a bunch of doo-doo. It's what those within the field of psychology call "becoming a product of a negative environment." Some time ago a gentleman practically boasted to me that if you came from a broken home and/or lived with adults addicted to alcohol or other drugs and/or were subjected to violent settings, there was a high percentage, as high as 90 percent, that you would act as you were, in a sense, *taught.* That there was basically no other option but to "continue the tradition" of affliction. That's not right! Now, for some folks who truly don't know any better or those who don't care about the future, yes, there is a *chance* they may fall into that negative "environmental trap." But if you can think for yourself, as I know you can, then you, and only you, can decide what you *are* and *are not* going to do with your life! If you are mocked and even harassed by others, be smart enough to look at the source and then ask yourself, "Are they happy? Are they a success? Or are *they* either deflecting their anguish onto others or stuck in their mire because of some *unresolved issue(s)?*"

Use Your Head

You are going to read this again and again and again until it becomes ingrained in your cranium: **Think for yourself!** Learn to distinguish fact from fiction, right from wrong. Better yourself by dealing with life's predicaments. Forge ahead. Choose wisely. And above all, in everything you do, *use your head!*

When it comes to problems, it's important to recognize the situations and then learn to deal with them as best as you can. Above all—and I repeat, *above all*—rise above the difficulties so as not to allow petty things, which you may have no control over anyhow, to consume your life!

With that stated, depending on the person and the situation, some folks aren't fully aware of what they're into until the predicament overtakes them. Working with young adults for many years, I've seen it with peer pressure, getting along with their parents, harboring feelings of animosity, dating, drugs, sex, to the pressures of passing semester finals. And while some things may seem invitingly adventurous, completely innocent, or fulfilling a curiosity about the darker side of beginning to develop a defensive, defiant attitude, you need to think about what you're getting into **before** you get into it. The key word being *think*. Don't be stupid enough to find yourself neck-deep in trouble before you realize you're in quicksand!

In my case, I realized as early as age four that I was out of step when it came to doing anything right to gain my mother's approval—whether it was making my bed good enough and fast enough, struggling to get dressed in the allotted time, laughing too loud, or even pronouncing words properly. Whenever I was alone with her, I'd always tense up, fumble my words, and spout off saying things that made no sense, or I'd ruin whatever I'd be in the middle of doing. For the most part, I did my best to bury my growing fear of Mother's disapproval or, worse, having to deal with her increasing wrath.

One Sunday afternoon I must have been playing too rough or making too much noise with my two brothers. Mother suddenly stormed into our room. My brothers, already conditioned to her mood swings, fled for cover while Mother proceeded to beat the life out of me. Having been subjected to this many times before, I had sense enough to cover myself, thinking it would all be over in a few seconds. But, for whatever the reason, Mother refused to let up.

It had been the end of a long, dreary weekend in which my brothers and I had been cooped up in the house since Friday due to bad weather. My father was a fireman who worked two twenty-four-hour back-to-back shifts, leaving my mother, a frustrated housewife, alone with her own unresolved issues and the solace of a droning black-and-white television set, with clouds of cigarette smoke hovering above her head and a drink nearby to calm her frayed nerves.

As Mother continued her assault, she suddenly lost her balance. She grabbed my left arm to regain her balance but fell on her behind just the same. It was just a slight popping sound coupled with a quick burning sensation, but by accident Mother had pulled my arm out of its socket. For a second I sat in shock. I simply couldn't believe "this" was happening to me. Yet the frightened look in her glazed eyes and Mother's gaped mouth made everything real. I knew it would only be a second before she rushed over to scoop me in her arms and rush me to the hospital. But without a word Mother changed her shocked expression, stood up, smoothed her smock dress, turned her back, and walked away. I knew she knew. All I could do was cradle my throbbing arm. I cried to myself, trapped in a fog of what had just transpired.

The *next* morning, after Father returned home and after hastily explaining that I had mysteriously fallen from the top bunk bed, Mother drove me to the hospital where she continued to spew in front of the hesitant doctor, only in more elaborate detail.

I knew right from wrong. A truth from a lie, yet I stood close to my mommy's leg as she had cried to my father and again in front of the doctor. Maybe, I fought to convince myself, it was only a strange accident that *I* had brought upon myself. *I* was playing loud. *I* broke the rules. *I* was always getting into trouble and deserved what *I* got. Anyway, I told myself, Mommy loves me, and it certainly can't get any worse. If I kept my mouth shut and my head down, somehow, I convinced myself, all of this would go away.

Thinking, hoping, and even praying for a problem to go away is not only absolutely unrealistic but foolish and, in some cases, dangerous.

Please understand, I am not in any way informing you about what happened to me for reasons of exploitation or sympathy. I am only stating through example how some situations, even at an early age or stage, can be a major problem before the person becomes fully aware of the predicament. At your age, if you think there may be a problem that you cannot solve by yourself, or if there is something that has been gnawing at you for some time, chances are that you need to get some help. Now.

Battle of the Psyche

Now, there are everyday things that all of us innocently put off until later—cleaning the room, doing homework, or the seemingly arduous chore of peeling away from the television for ten seconds to take out the trash. But have you noticed that even when you're watching a show or hanging out with friends as the homework piles up, you can't fully relax? You feel this pressure build and build. And no matter how much you do your best to avoid the issue, the longer you do, the more that pressure intensifies. What causes this? It is basically your conscience battling with *what you're doing* compared with what *you should do*.

Another indication of not addressing problems is: Have you ever wondered why you may lose a good night's sleep? Part of the reason may be that your brain is replaying your unsolved problem over and over because, like a computer, it's simply trying to find a solution to the problem and will not rest until it does. Simple advice: Rather than avoid situations, develop the *habit* of addressing them as they come up.

Look at it this way: If you have a bad flu and after taking medicine you only become more ill, what should you do? Answer: Get help. You see a doctor; most likely the doctor will spend only a few minutes with you, quickly diagnose the extent of the problem, and prescribe specific medication. Within a short time you're back on your feet. If your car is not running as it should and, after tinkering with it to no avail (with my luck it only gets worse), what's the next logical step? You take it to a professional mechanic who, probably with a few turns of a screwdriver or a wrench, fixes your car just like that. If you can't seem to grasp a polynomial from basic algebra, you get assistance from your teacher or a tutor.

Get the picture? The thing is, most problems are relatively simple and easy to fix *if addressed in their early stages*. But if brushed aside, especially if a habit of doing so has already been formed, the issues can develop into something worse, to the point that they overwhelm the initial problem. In math if you do not have a good handle on polynomials, how can you advance to understanding a quadratic equation? And, again, this is only *basic* algebra.

Now, have you noticed that some of your problems began to amplify during the same time that you began to shut out those close to you? Part of this is normal, and I know and fully appreciate that at your age, for reasons of privacy, there are a great number of things you keep to yourself. But let me ask you this: When was the last time you actually sat down with your parents, your guardians, or an adult in whom you trust and brought up a predicament you were struggling with? If it has been a while, be honest and ask yourself why. Why have you held off? What's holding you back? What are you truly afraid of, ridicule or rejection? Or maybe you think you're the only one who's ever faced this issue.

Please, whatever you do, *don't* clam up. That *is* one of the most damaging things you can do against yourself. Trust me, you're not alone. Everybody—and I mean *everybody*—may feel some initial embarrassment or a little anxiety when coming to terms with seeking guidance. What you may be feeling is completely normal.

Whatever you do, don't fall into the trap of developing a habit of trying to run away or bury your problems.

Know this: In the short term, maybe, just maybe, brushing problems aside or burying your problems may buy you some time, but that's all. Sooner or later you will have to address these situations. And, again, simply brushing things aside or wishing for a problem to go away is not only unrealistic but also idiotic and, in some cases, dangerous. *Now,* do something to help yourself before it's too late.

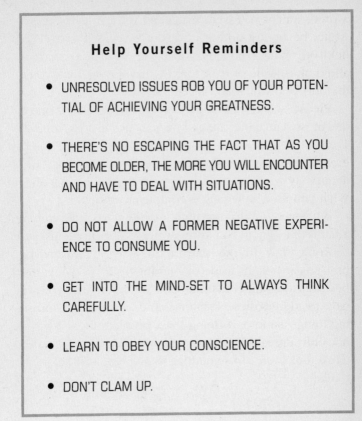

Help Yourself Reminders

- UNRESOLVED ISSUES ROB YOU OF YOUR POTEN-
  TIAL OF ACHIEVING YOUR GREATNESS.

- THERE'S NO ESCAPING THE FACT THAT AS YOU
  BECOME OLDER, THE MORE YOU WILL ENCOUNTER
  AND HAVE TO DEAL WITH SITUATIONS.

- DO NOT ALLOW A FORMER NEGATIVE EXPERI-
  ENCE TO CONSUME YOU.

- GET INTO THE MIND-SET TO ALWAYS THINK
  CAREFULLY.

- LEARN TO OBEY YOUR CONSCIENCE.

- DON'T CLAM UP.

Chapter 3

It's Not Necessarily You

There are some problems, primarily ones not dealt with, that eventually become so huge that they reach a point where they have to be addressed. To handle problems properly you must—I repeat, *must*—fully come to terms with them and rid yourself of the situation no matter how enormous or disgusting the problem may be. The situation itself can eventually be the most positive turning point of your life.

This concept is so vital that I'll state it again: There are instances when, at that particular time, it may be the worst thing that happens to you, but in the long run it just may evolve into something that changes your life for the better forever!

Because of my extensive traveling, giving lectures, and interviewing scores of people over the years, rarely does a day pass that I am not asked the question (mainly from inquiring "young adults" who seek a straight answer): "What was the turning point in your life, Dave?" I have to state honestly that besides the obvious—the day when I was blessed and taken away from my mother and then made a ward of the court—for me the turning point evolved from a detestable, terrifying situation which began as a building block that not only saved my life but became *my foundation* for facing, solving, and defeating major problems ever since.

It had taken me four years, but by the time I was eight years old I became fully aware of the ever-changing intensity of how Mother treated me. I knew there was a dramatic, almost theatrical difference when either my father was home from work or my brothers were nearby, compared to the cold, sometimes sadistic way Mother treated me when I was alone with her. And yet, as much as I viewed life in a simplistic black-and-white, right-from-wrong world, I still kept my increasing anxiety to myself.

One afternoon, as Mother screamed nonstop at me in her drunken state over the "utter humiliation of disgracing the family name" by receiving a letter from Santa Claus, who reprimanded me for my horrible behavior and the enormous toll it had placed on my fragile mother. For obvious reasons (Santa Claus? Yeah, right), I knew it was a hoax, especially since Mother waved the papers in front of me that displayed her distinctive cursive handwriting.

And *still* I never said a word. I took my punishment. Part of me felt that I was in a sense "the common denominator" for all the problems within the family. Yet another part of me wanted to cling to the fleeting hope that my mommy would wake up from her vengeful personality so we could both live happily ever after.

Later, when Mother informed my inebriated, passive father and my concerned brothers one Sunday afternoon that I was no longer a member of the family—that my name was not allowed to be spoken and I was now banished to live in the basement and sleep on a World War II army cot—I simply lowered my head in shame and accepted my fate. After four years of escalating tensions and knowing no other way of life, part of me believed I deserved such treatment. But yet my inner voice began to take over, telling me how wrong all of this was.

So, as commanded, as trained by my mother, as a form of humiliation and punishment, I shivered in the cold basement, sitting on my hands with my head tilted backward. No matter how bad the throbbing pain was that crept up to my neck, out of fear of further retribution I refused to do anything for myself that would help me ease some of my pain. Whenever I wasn't praying that the monstrous serpents I imagined slithering within the dark didn't eat me alive, I *still* tried to convince myself that my situation couldn't possibly become any worse. As much as I knew how wrong everything was, I *still* held on to a wish that any day, even any moment, Mother would realize her anger against me was all a mistake and we would somehow put all of this behind us.

Let me stop here for a moment. If you or anyone you know may be in a harmful situation, I beg of you: **Get some help.** Be adult enough to use your head and do the right thing. As dramatic as this may sound: **Save a life!**

You're at the age to realize that nobody's perfect. We all say and do things, especially when we're upset, that we don't mean to. That's a fact of life. Hopefully we learn from our errors, not repeat them, and move on to more productive ways. But you're also at the age and maturity level to understand right from wrong. When it comes to circumstances, such as abuse in any form, that's no way to live and no one, I repeat, **no one**—deserves to be treated in that manner.

If you or anybody you know is in a harmful situation, usually the situation only becomes worse, unless there's a drastic change with both individuals. The person on the receiving end of this treatment, whatever their justification, may be confused and conflicted with a whirlwind of mixed emotions, forcing that person to do nothing for themselves. **This** is no way to live. Again, if you or anybody you know and care for cannot solve a particular problem themselves, help them by **getting them some help!**

I owe you an apology. For as much as I repeat myself and seemingly berate you with my instructions, to tell you the truth (as if you haven't figured it out already), back then I never did anything for myself. I never spoke up, let alone confront my tormentor. I never told anyone. I took whatever Mother threw my way. Why? One reason was that things were very different back then. In many households in my time, the ultimate swear word was to state the word *no* to any adult. Back then whenever a parent commanded "jump," as a kid you'd immediately ask, "How high?" A child never questioned their parents' authority. Children were in the background, hence the saying that children should be *seen but not heard*. I'm not saying that back then things were bad; no, not at all. It was simply a little more restrictive. Maybe because of those times people like myself are less authoritative now, and more open to addressing things. Again, in many cases when something bad happens, something more positive can come out of it.

Another reason that I didn't do anything for myself may have been from a form of control or brainwashing. As a small child I felt there was always this one kid in the family who was slow or stupid and always got in trouble. I just happened to be that kid. In the beginning I didn't know I was being controlled; again, it all seemed so normal. At the time I strongly felt there was no one to seek guidance from and nowhere to go. In childlike terms, I felt this was simply my lot in life. But times are different now. There are a multitude of resources for help if only *you* are willing to take the first step and do something for yourself. My main point to you in these preceding paragraphs and throughout this entire book is this: **Learn from my mistakes.**

Back then, with all that I didn't do for myself, a situation arose that somehow forced me to do something proactive, and as horrible and disgusting as it was at the time, I'm now *thankful* in a certain light that it happened. For it definitely changed my entire outlook on my life.

Pay close attention.

I was eight years old when one afternoon, as my father worked at the fire station and my two brothers were away at a Boy Scout meeting, Mother began as she always did with me—standing ramrod straight like a statue in the center of the kitchen as she unloaded an endless list of felonies I committed that particular day even though I had just come home from school. Between her drinks came the usual statements: "You're the reason your father and I don't get along. You're the reason I can't be happy. I hate the sound of your voice. I hate the way you look. I wish you had never been born. I wish you were dead. I hate you. I hate you. I hate you!"

Look at the Source!

I'm going to pause here for a moment to tell you something extremely important. If you ever come across anyone who makes a habit of running folks down while they're jabbing a finger in your face, look where the finger is connected. In other words, look at the source. Then ask yourself some questions: Is that person who is spouting off happy? Is that person a success? Is that person a positive role model? Chances are that person is not.

Another thing to remember is that when those same kind of folks (unlike those of us who may simply be having a bad day) state things like "I hate you. I think you're ugly. You're stupid" or whatever hurtful articulation that spews from their seedy mouth, what they're **really** saying, what they **truly** mean is: "I hate myself. I feel ugly. I feel stupid. I hate my life. *I wish I were dead.*"

It's called *projection*. For whatever the reason, folks who are jealous, upset at themselves, deeply hurt (from unresolved issues), or very incensed on how their life turned out *project* their animosity onto others. Why? It has been my experience that folks who have given up on themselves (again, through their own actions or inactions) are absolutely and completely miserable. And sometimes the only joy in their life is when they can put down or spread their cancer of hate to others.

There are some folks who project their bitterness or fear through nothing more than ignorance. They're not nessarily bad folks, but just by being empty-headed or for a host of other reasons they project their ill feelings onto you. Why? You're young, you're fast, you have these, these *ideas,* wild ideas, radical notions. You dress oddly at best while listening to music so extreme and at such blistering volumes that it can make a dog's ears bleed. You're different!

Bottom line: At your age you *will* come across those who will treat you unjustly, and it will most likely cut you to the bone. As a young teen in foster care I had moved from the dilapidated "wrong side of the tracks" type of home, which I never thought was all that bad considering what I had endured as a kid with my mother, into a *Leave It to Beaver*–style neighborhood. Within days I had set my sights on a beautiful young lass, marched up to her immaculate stately-like house, and almost, just inches away, nearly made my first lip-lock when out of nowhere the Cruella De Vil of moms shoved my soon-to-be future love of my life aside and blasted me with every possible put-down known to man: I'm nothing. I'm street vermin. I'm a disgusting sight. I'm a hooligan. What in heaven's name did *I* do to become a foster child? I'm never, ever going to amount to anything. I'm never going to make it. I'm nothing but trailer trash. And above all, I should stick to *my own kind.*

Wow.

Being a several-year veteran of the ins and outs of the foster care system, I had heard all those words in many various combinations a gazillion times before. But that time, at that vulnerable moment in my life when I felt good enough about myself to build up the courage to step out of my comfort zone and walk upright, head held high, absorbing the everyday beauty of the neighborhood, to have the rare opportunity for a geek like me to look directly into the eyes of a pretty girl and just talk to her, every syllable of Ms. De Vil's put-down tone was like a sledgehammer beating me into the ground. By the time I retreated down the street, I felt I was an inch tall. Yet the one thing that made me boil inside was the fact that prissy-priss Cruella didn't know anything about me. Okay, sure, on the outside I wore a goofy worn-out red and black flannel long-sleeved shirt that was easily two sizes too small. I had overgrown, shaggy, straggly hair, broken black-frame glasses, slouched posture, and I stuttered uncontrollably when I became nervous, which was quite often. But on the inside—where Cruella and others like her didn't care to scrutinize—I had already overcome more in my young life than they could possibly imagine in any one of their lifetimes. Rather than cop out and cave in on myself, as I had already seen so many other teens my age do, I always wanted to make something of myself. Something, anything, just as long as I bettered myself to live a life free of fear, ridicule, and violence. I just wanted to be happy, to live life on my terms. Nothing more, nothing grand. Just to be happy was enough for me.

No excuses. No one handing me anything except something *I* could achieve. I knew full well with my luck I'd probably have to jump through every hoop and walk through every minefieldlike maze of life. But that was okay with me. As much as I wanted things to be easier, part of me wouldn't have it any other way. I would do *my* best. I'd hold true to *my* cause for my reasons and not for the pleasure or *possible* acceptance of others. And no matter what others saw of me or how they instantly judged me, as much as I strayed, fumbled, and just plain screwed up, I knew who *I* was and the person *I* wanted to be.

Start Looking at You!

As much as I tell you to look at the source of what others say and do, I want you to start looking, start probing, and pick up that shovel to your soul and dig. Dig deep, real deep into the source within you. When push comes to shove, as things will, carefully acknowledge the situation for what it is, but count on yourself to turn things around. For **you** to make something positive, anything, no matter how small or insignificant it may be to others, keep your faith with yourself.

I know this sounds kinda stupid, but trust me when I say: Every dog has its day. If you stay the course, if you remain true to you, even with all the slander, all the most hurtful words or deeds thrown your way by stupid, idiotic people, you, my dear friend, will rise above it all. In time you **will** be a better, wiser, and far more compassionate person. Keep your eye on the ball and look at your source when these misdeeds are being unjustly done to you. And you never know, maybe someday those same folks will be singing a different tune.

For me it was something straight out of the movies. By sheer coincidence many years later, when still flying for the United States Air Force, I met up with Ms. De Vil. During a private moment she confessed that having been raised in a fairly well-to-do family and being then a young, naive mother, she believed, for some unexplainable reason, that foster children had committed something unspeakable in order to be "placed" as a ward of the court. That afternoon years ago, when she emptied both barrels of spew in my face, she admitted she was only looking out for her children. Sitting next to her now and seeing the emotion and sincere regret on her face, I nodded in agreement. As a young father of a precious, beautiful, preschool boy, I was *extremely* protective of him. Yet what blew me away was when this lady gently took my hand and with mist in her eyes apologized for saying such horrible things, for willingly going out of her way to hurt my feelings. She went on to state that not a day had passed since our initial encounter when she did not carry shame for acting as she did. In all, the once overly protective, gullible mother stated she was just stupid and acted out of ignorance. And now because we cleared the air between us, this once stuffy, arrogant, well-to-do snob is one of my biggest fans, and after all these years we still remain in close contact. I'm proud to say that every Mother's Day the former Ms. De Vil receives a large bouquet of flowers from my office.

Remember, all of us say things in the heat of the moment. None of us are faultless. However, as hard as it is for me to state this, there are people who are not like Mr. and Mrs. De Vil, who are just crass, who live for nothing more than to vomit their pain onto others, particularly onto those like yourself who are on the cusp of independence and have their entire life in front of them. As sickening as this sounds, their only pleasure, their only satisfaction is to degrade, dehumanize, or suck any happiness or chances of success from anyone they can. It's the honest-to-God truth.

Don't get sucked in. Don't let some pointless, hateful statements from some asshole fill your head. If such statements have filled your head in the past, I want you to flush that junk away . . . just as you do when you go to the bathroom. Get rid of it and don't look back. Again, look where that finger is connected. Look at these people and the life they live. **Look at the source!**

The source in front of me went on stating, "You've made my life a living hell. Now I'm going to show you what hell is like!" Mother then snatched my right hand, turned on the gas stove, and held my right arm over the flames for several seconds. Between the sensations of watching my arm, smelling the hairs from my arm burn, and hearing the sound of my screaming, I almost couldn't believe all of this was happening to me.

Finally Mother let go, and I tumbled to the floor, licking my reddening arm and blackened hairs. Above me I could hear Mother faintly rant, "Look at this mess! Look at my dress! How in the *hell* am I going to get rid of that smell?"

Without hesitation I cradled my throbbing arm, and with tears rolling down my cheeks I now cried out to the one person I longed to love me. "I'm sorry," I sobbed. "I'm sorry for the mess. I'll clean it up. I'm sorry 'bout you and Dad. I'm sorry for makin' you mad, about gettin' into trouble. I'm sorry . . . for . . . everything. I'm sorry!"

Looking back at that incident in my life, thinking again in childlike black-and-white terms, I had somehow fought to convince myself that if I said I was sorry—and not just utter the words but declare from the bottom of my heart how horrible I felt for all the suffering I had caused Mother, Father, my brothers, my relatives, those at school, the neighborhood, and the whole world—a gazillion million times, Mother would have to forgive me. She would have to know how much I was still reaching out to her— that, above everything, I was worthy of her love. Even with everything she did against me, it somehow made me want her acceptance all the more.

For Some the World's Not Enough

As you have probably already realized, you can have straight A's in school, associate yourself with clean-cut aspiring friends, never smoke or drink, let alone look at anyone with a gleam in your eyes, never have an impure thought, work full-time after school and then return home and cook, clean, mow the yard, and pick all the dog poop known to mankind, do your homework late into the night, be the kindest person there is who is more than willing to lend a hand, a hug, or a kind word, and for some folks you're *still not good enough*. It's as if *you* can do nothing right in their eyes, as if *you're* the one who *still* needs to prove yourself to them.

Wrong!

Know this: You can carry feelings of great sorrow and be willing to go to the corners of the world to make things right, and it's still not enough for those you're trying to please. You can humbly present these people with the cure for cancer, AIDS, the common cold, and all diseases known to mankind on a silver platter, and then feed, clothe, and house everyone on the planet, and *still* you're the one who feels you could do more, who should do more. You think if you did still more, then maybe, just maybe you'd be worthy of their acceptance, their praise, or, Lord willing, their love.

On the other side of the coin, I cannot begin to tell you of the thousands of young adults I've had the privilege of meeting who have unfortunately been brutalized, molested, and treated like garbage, and yet they are the ones who feel it's all their fault, that they somehow brought the situation on themselves. Some cling to a deluded notion that if they had confessed their well of sorrow over the situation, if they had done something different, anything, to change how others felt about them, then somehow these poor souls wouldn't have brought on all this hideous suffering.

Wrong again!

The truth of the matter is there are a lot of very sick people in the world. There are some situations you have no control over. There are instances where, through no fault of your own, you find yourself in the middle, and you have no idea how you got there. And no matter what you say or how much you do to prove your worthiness to others, it will all be in vain.

Do not—I repeat, *do not*—fall into the trap of thinking everything's your fault, that you deserve to be treated like scum. No, no, no, **no!**

And please, I beg you, don't even think about giving your best away to "so-and-so" or attempting to act in "such-and-such" manner for the mere hope that others might become impressed, like, or accept you as an individual. *And* don't get caught up in trying to become a member of that super-hot, ultra-cool, end-all-be-all, prissy, best-dressed, badass posse, clique, or group that roams the hallways showing off to everyone and no one. Who delusionally believe they own the school, the local mall, or the outer regional wastelands of Tiny Town, USA. And when they strut, stroll, or swagger by, others (they believe) who are at the bottom rung on the social food chain should either whither, melt, or bow their heads in awe. The reality is, no matter how you act or what you say or do for them, they still won't like, respect, or accept you, let alone allow you into the fold or even give you the time of day. **Reality check. Get real!**

In all the history of history, doing for others in the craving of their acceptance never pans out and only degrades you in the process. I should know. Look what I did as a child when I lived with Mother as her "basement slave." I performed the endless laundry list of chores in record time, brought home near-perfect grades from elementary school, and, as commanded by her, made sure I didn't look up at her, speak unless spoken to first, let alone go to the bathroom without first seeking permission, all the while enduring the never-ending siege of beatings and any other sinister "games" she threw my way. It didn't matter how long I was choked by her, starved, beaten, or degraded, with every new day I'd think maybe, just maybe, my own mother might hold off on one less punch to the face, one less kick to my body, or one less stomp to my face when I lay crumpled on the floor—and that somehow translated in my twisted mind to "she *liked me*."

Now, as much as I advised you in your life, tell me who's the one who was stupidly stupid? However, as you already know, in life there are a lot of folks who'll do anything just for the mere chance of being liked, wanted, or loved. Not one of us is perfect. All of us make mistakes and do stupid, stupid things. But just remember: No matter the circumstance or situation, we are in fact **all too human.**

All I ask of you is to learn from my mistakes and from those of others and your own blunders. Don't keep throwing yourself away, making a bad situation far worse and in some cases dangerously so. Don't paint yourself into a corner from which you can't escape. Why? Because paint is messy and takes a long, long time to dry, and when you try to sneak away from it, you're only left with footprints of regret for you and everyone else to see and to always remember.

As for me, I stupidly went from bad to worse. During my first few years as a young, gullible, no-esteem, socially starved teenager, especially immediately after I was rescued and placed in foster care, I cannot begin to relate to you how overwhelming the sudden need was for *me* to fit in, be part of a group, and have others like me—really, really like me! At one point, while still coming to terms with barely surviving those years of degradation and isolation, I quickly discovered I had no building blocks to guide me on everyday social nuances—from basic communication, let alone slang words, to the sudden importance of fashion, to interacting with kids my age, and to displaying common courtesy to adults. I was completely, utterly lost. I will not even begin to go into the anxiety of attempting to speak to someone of the opposite sex. With every passing day, as I learned more about my new world, the more I dreamt and the more I salivated for wanting to be wanted.

In a matter of months my desperation and immaturity got the best of me. I discovered myself acting in arrogant ways, saying and doing things that I knew weren't who I really was on the inside. But, hey, I didn't care, just as long as I was appreciated or needed; that's all that mattered. It got to the point that I clung to a low-end, disgruntled bunch of preteen wannabe rebellious punks who basically had no problems except too much time on their hands. But when they wanted something, anything at all, that's when I suddenly became indispensable, Mr. Popular, the go-to guy. No matter what I was doing or how mad or humiliated I was from being lied to, ditched, teased, and even beaten up by "my friends" just days before, whenever they snapped their fingers or rode their bikes over to my foster home, all was instantly forgiven, all was forgotten, based on the glimmer of a chance that today just might be the day that I would finally be accepted.

I lied, cheated, acted pompous, humiliated myself, and stole. I nabbed anything possible. In the beginning I convinced myself it was all harmless fun, just a few candy bars and some ice cream cones. Then it became toys of all shapes and sizes. Next I graduated to music records and clothes. Sure, sometimes I was seen literally fleeing the scene, only to be caught by a faster security guard who nabbed me by my waistband before threatening to call the police. But *I* wasn't scared. Hell no. *Friends* don't "rat out"; if anything, protecting my "mates" would only elevate my position within the group, make them appreciate me all the more. Or so I naively believed.

Bottom line: All "my friends" wanted from me was all I could give them and all they could squeeze out of me.

When I eventually landed in juvenile hall, in part for running away from my foster home out of fear after my "best buddy" started a fire at the local school, which I put out, it was after spending a lot of days lying on a thin mattress in a urine-tainted cell that I began to ponder my actions and what I had brought upon myself. While lying on my back in the middle of the night in the stale eight-by-four-foot room, I replayed all the countless times those folks—who always seemed to aggravate me the most; who tore into me for hours upon hours until my ears bled. Those folks pleading, begging, crying for me to wise up. Those people wasting *my* time—teachers, foster parents, my social worker, and even my older foster siblings reaching out and warning me before I skated out too far on the thin ice. One cold, lonely night I figured out, duh, *they* were not my enemy, *they* weren't trying to use me, and, duh, *they* were only acting in my best interest for the sole purpose of trying to protect me from myself for my own damn good. **Duh!**

My own good.

For your own damn good. I hope and pray you get the lesson I'm trying to convey to you. When you give yourself away, you end up with nothing except an empty shell of your former self.

The things I did back then were beyond stupid. And today, as a father of a young man about your age and as much as I try to be a positive mentor to you, I'm very ashamed of my past actions. I truly am. No matter what happened to me or against me up until that point, I and I alone was responsible for the misdeeds I performed. Sure, I could have tried to squirm my way out of it by boldly stating, "Well, because such and such happened to me . . .

because I'm mad at the world . . . or so-and-so made me do it, but that wouldn't be right. And it certainly wouldn't be truthful, for I knew right from wrong. Again, I believe if you can get dressed in the morning all by yourself, then you are capable of making your own decisions. And in today's world, if I attempted any of those defiant acts, I would deservingly be locked up and put away for a long, long time.

All in the name of wanting to be wanted.

Part of my yearning was because I felt lost, confused, and overwhelmed, just like a lot of young adults today. Part of my desperate longing was for my mother's love and acceptance—the same sick individual who constantly degraded and tortured me with relish for her own twisted amusement that almost left me dead several times. The same person who brainwashed me all those years—that everything in her life was my fault, that I was never good enough . . . Umm. My mother, the source of the miserable person who acted out because of her source, who in turn may have acted out because of that person's source . . . Who in turn . . .

Do you see the pattern here?

Pretty disturbing, eh?

Again, to make certain you get this: Everybody makes mistakes. All of us at one time or another act out in ways for whatever reason. Some good, some bad. But *now* when you act in a way that is not in your best interest, for the reason of appeasing others, I want you to stop, think, and look at *your* source and ask yourself why in the hell you are **reacting** that way.

Examine your source before you "go off" and develop the habit of doing something that can detract from your greatness for the rest of your life. Giving your best away for the sole purpose of overly appeasing others who wouldn't give you the time of day is only going to hurt you in the process. And that's a fact! And, as stated before, **you are better than that.**

Again, I fully understand, respect, and appreciate that at your age and with all the social pressures going on around you it's so easy to cave in—especially if you are like me at your age and have low self-esteem or are going through issues. But all that's going to happen are two things: 1) You will feed into these people's sick little games, and 2) *you* would have allowed yourself to be used. And if not recognized and dealt with, this can become a disturbing and dominating lifestyle.

Put this in your back pocket: *People will **do** you if you're **doable**—*mentally, physically, sexually, spiritually, financially, you name it. Get what I'm saying? I don't mean to sound crude, but it's true. I don't mean to beat a dead horse here, but this is important: There are folks who crave nothing more than to take advantage of anyone they can for as long as they can. If you fall into the habit of thinking you're the only one to blame or throwing yourself needlessly at others, then tell me, whose life are *you* living? But, hey, the trade-off is—maybe, maybe, maybe—that there's the slight chance these folks might possibly like you. Wow! What a deal!

Besides, after high school when you're out on your own in the real world working full-time, going to college or continuation school, raising your babies, paying taxes, gassing up your car before running to the grocery store, does it really matter what some kids or that twisted person who spewed those vomitlike sentences thought of you or what they said against you? Is any of that really going to matter? **It damn well shouldn't!**

There's a lot of garbage out there in the world, and some people and some things are inevitably negative. There's no escaping it. It's simply another cold fact of life. *It's how you deal with all that life throws at you that really matters.* Your life, your choice. You can feed into it by either duplicating onto others what happened to you or, through your own choice, feel inferior and act out, or you can be mature enough and wise enough to know manure from flowers by standing tall, using your head, and examining the source!

Help Yourself Reminders

- THE LONGER YOU PROCRASTINATE, THE WORSE YOUR PROBLEMS BECOME.

- WHEN OTHERS ARE POINTING *THAT* FINGER OF DEFEAT YOUR WAY, BEFORE YOU BUY INTO THEIR ADVICE, LOOK AT THE SOURCE!

- DON'T APPEASE OTHERS WHO DON'T CARE ABOUT YOU, MUCH LESS THEMSELVES.

Chapter 4

The Fear Factor

I couldn't believe my ears. Mother's command almost made me pee on myself. Still on my knees on the kitchen's multicolored spotted floor cradling my burnt throbbing arm, I was still trying to process Mother screaming above me, "How in the hell am I going to get rid of that smell?" when everything seemed to suddenly become silent.

Breaking a cardinal rule of never setting eyes on Mother unless granted permission, I stole a glance at my tormentor. With her hands glued to her hips and pulsating darkened cheeks on her red face, Mother seemed more like a wild bull about to charge. All that was missing was the smoke escaping her nostrils.

Still in shock, I wanted nothing more than to close my eyes and disappear. I wanted to transform myself into some micro-sized insect and hide within the tall green grass, while praying that the gas in the stove would run out.

My little diversion lasted only a mere second. *"Do . . . you . . . not . . . hear . . . me?"* Mother slowly and distinctively pronounced. "I said, I want you to stand up, go over to the gas stove, then lay down on it and burn for me."

My chest seemed to tighten, and I did all that I could not to pass out. My mind kept racing with the singular thought *This is it* over and over again. I had no choice. I had to obey her just as I always had. She was "the Mother," she was right, and I was the one who deserved to be punished. Somehow *this* was all my fault. Somehow I had brought all of this upon myself.

But I didn't do anything. I knew in my heart that I did not commit the latest set of atrocities Mother now claimed—that at lunchtime while at school Mother had spied me playing on the grass, which was the crime of crimes. This whole thing was wrong and went way beyond being punched if I laughed too loud, if I couldn't tie my shoes properly, or stuttering when I became nervous and locked up in front of Mother. In some weird sense I became transfixed on the gas stove's orange-purple flame and its distinctive hiss from the burner. I began to repeat: "This is wrong. I don't deserve this. This is so, so wrong."

An overwhelming fear began to creep up my spine. For years I had known—yet I still did nothing for myself, for which I hated myself, and now for my inactions—Mother was going to kill me. The more I kept staring at the flames, the more terrified I became. With perfect clarity I could visualize myself lying on the flickering stove, and I knew full well that if I did as Mother commanded, I was indeed going to perish. I was going to die.

My entire being became focused on the singular thought of lying still on the gas stove as ordered by Mother and burning to death. Even the pulsating pain from my right arm seemed to fade away. I took in a deep breath. While avoiding Mother's frame, my eyes darted in every direction. My ears caught the attention of the clicking sound of the electric clock that hung above the doorway in the kitchen. In my excited state I drew in another breath while staring at the clock that read 3:50 in the afternoon. For some reason I stated the time to myself again: "Ten minutes till four o'clock. Ten minutes till four . . ."

Suddenly it came to me. *"Time!"* my brain screamed. My two brothers come home from their Boy Scout meeting precisely at four o'clock, and Mother never acts this bizarre in front of them or my father. So if I can just slow her down, if I can beg, borrow, steal, and buy just ten minutes' worth of time, then maybe today I won't die!

That last sentence began the turning point of my life. I want to stop here for a moment and dissect that last sentence again. At that age, at that moment in time, I felt that rather than caving in and giving up to a definite outcome—as I had for years due to brainwashing and habit—if I could *instead do* something, anything, meaning that *I* take the offensive, then maybe, just maybe Mother wouldn't kill me.

Again, all of us face situations. In the more serious ones, when push comes to shove you can freeze and allow things to happen to you or against you, knowing full well the outcome, *or* you can take the offensive, take the slightest initiative, and **do** something for yourself.

Even as I write these words, there is little doubt that had I not taken some form of action, my mother—a deviant, seemingly possessed individual—had every intention of killing me that afternoon. It took my being scared of that possible outcome that finally forced me to **do** something.

Are You Scared?

Please take a second and answer this question out loud: *Have you ever been scared?*

Of course you have. All of us have been at one time or another. If you answered yes, I want to thank you for your honesty. I know it's never easy to let down your guard. To do so takes a lot of guts.

However, if you immediately boasted to yourself, "Man, I never get scared. I ain't scared of nothin'," you're either lying or stupidly trying to fool yourself. Grow up and realize a fact of life. The toughest folks in the world become scared: single parents who bust their behinds every day to ensure that their children are well kept and off the streets, those fighting with every fiber of their being to overcome life-threatening illnesses, and everyday people who seemingly have it all together. What they all have in common is they muster that inner strength or whatever courage they can scrape together and turn whatever disabling fear they have into *their advantage*. That's what makes them and you strong.

Look at a man who was literally in the middle of it all and yet kept it together when our country was under attack that terrible day in September 2001, a gentleman widely known as Captain Courageous, the former mayor of New York City, Rudy Giuliani. He stated, "You have to know what you believe if you are going to get through a crisis. It's feeling fear and then figuring out how to move through it and get done what you have to get done. Courage is not the person with the ability to run into a burning building or save a drowning child, *but* the individual with the selflessness to manage their fears to do those acts." And this from a man who had already battled cancer and who became temporarily trapped in a nearby building after one of the World Trade Center towers collapsed. A sentence by Mr. Giuliani puts that tragic morning into focus: "September 11th to me marks the first day America actually became safer because now we can see reality."

Bottom line: **You** take that ordeal and flip it around, then use it to propel you forward! Use your fear to the point it gives you an intense focus that thrusts you beyond what you were fearful of in the first place!

And part of that powerful inner drive is a strong emphasis of *what **you are doing*** physically, mentally, and spiritually *in your everyday life.*

I know this may sound a little odd, but being a little scared at this stage in your life is not a bad thing. If that's what it takes to keep you on course, then I want you to be a little scared. If the word *scared* is, well, too *frightening* for you, then maybe a better term is *concerned.* I want you to be concerned about what's going on in your life. I want you to maintain a certain discernment about how you *act,* what you do, what you wear, what you say, what you think, and how you treat yourself and others around you. I want you to be concerned about who you hang out with, what they do, their values, and their goals and dreams. Be concerned about every class in school and every test you take. Be concerned about taking responsibility for things rather than copping out, blaming others, making excuses, or taking the easy way out.

And you had better be concerned about the serious implications of becoming "a little bit pregnant," becoming a teen father, becoming a slave to drugs, or living out every day of the rest of your life in misery if you "ain't scared of nothin' " or if you feel "it" couldn't happen to you. If you're successful in fooling yourself, one day you'll look back on those days when you *acted* so tough, were so cool, were too much of a badass to be *concerned* about what was going on around you, and then ask yourself: Was it worth it? As you read these words, and if you can still lie to yourself that you never get scared, well then my hat's off to you, for you had better be tough to live a pitiful, hollow life—all because you were too "whatever" to be scared, concerned, or give a fleeting thought to how things might turn out.

Wake up!

Don't Tempt Fate

Don't be stupid! Don't fall into the trap that "it" could never happen to you. Fact: Sooner or later "it" catches up with you. And "it" can happen when you least expect "it." And "it" always does so with a vengeance.

Have you ever seen someone stupidly throw caution to the wind one too many times? Do you want to put your life into the hands of that person who always drinks too much and then insists on driving you home? "Hey, man. Hop in. Don't worry, I do this all the time." Do you want to be with that person who tries to convince you that you can't get pregnant the first time? Or do you feel you have to prove yourself to be with that person or act a certain way to be allowed within that group? Have you seen those in school who, for whatever reason or excuse, just don't care about anything, lose interest in class, and then, to no surprise, their grades plummet, and you know before they do how things are going to turn out? Duh!

Simply stated, *they lack regard*. They lack *maturity*. They lack *courage*. Courage to face the issues. The guts to take a stand. The valor to do the right thing for the right reason. To deal with situations as best as you can and walk out the other side a better person.

The Good Scare

For the record, I say that being a little scared or a little concerned is a very positive thing. Now don't become terrified to the point that it prevents you from doing anything in your life. Instead, use your concern to keep you away from the pitfalls and minefields of life.

Being scared just might save your life, just as it did a young nine-year-old girl who was brazenly kidnapped from her home when she returned one afternoon from school. Not only did this brave young girl begin to formulate an escape plan when she overheard the kidnapper discussing exactly how he would dispose of "the body," but after the perpetrator became spooked and released her, she had the sense to keep it together and recall the key detail that led to the arrest of the individual by way of a local pizza delivery service that dropped off the food at the house where she was held captive.

Being scared, concerned, guarded—or whatever word you choose—keeps you focused and keeps everything in perspective—just as it did that courageous young girl.

In fact, there are those in the field of psychology who state that a certain amount of anxiety is very healthy.

Being concerned about things makes you less complacent, less vulnerable to serious problems, not only in school but in your health, relationships, work, finances, and just about every aspect of your life.

Another way of looking at it is: Have you ever been sick and had to take medication that made you perk right up, but then after a while you became a little passive, lost your focus, and weren't too concerned when you "forgot" to take your medicine, only to have a relapse that was far worse than being sick the first time? If you know anyone who lives with diabetes, a heart condition, high blood pressure, or any other serious illness, then you know just how critical the penalty can be for that lack of regard.

The bottom line: A little bit of apprehension in your life is not a bad thing. It keeps you on track and prevents you from drifting off course when it comes to what you want to achieve. Being concerned is never a sign of weakness; it is the mark of an individual who is mature enough and has the mental strength to face up to situations when others run for cover. Even in the heat of the moment when everything seems impossible, being a little scared helps you focus and discover the way out of the worst situations.

One day when I was a teenager still in foster care, while strolling through the local park with my two friends, Paul and David, a group of older tough kids jumped me and tried to take my cheap yet prized boom box. After trying to evade the group by backing up, which didn't work, while attempting to talk my way out of my predicament, I ended up getting my butt kicked all the more. All I could do was hang on to my prized radio for dear life. I lasted a whole ten seconds before the head bully wrapped his bulging arm around my skinny neck, making me pass out.

I regained consciousness with a pounding sensation in my head telling me I was not dreaming, while my eyes adjusted to the group of bullies who thrust my radio high in the air like some kind of trophy from the days of Roman gladiators. Suddenly, for no logical reason, I sprung up, shimmied my way through the throng of thugs, and begged the leader to "please, please, please let me have my radio back." For a second the ruffian smiled. He gave me a slight nod. I felt he understood. He knew how much my Christmas present meant to me. Seconds later, like some ballet dancer, with fluid grace he spun around, leaned back, and placed a perfect backspin kick into my face, launching me into the air. I crashed with a thud and passed out yet again, but not before the entire gang took turns kicking me from every direction.

In the middle of the stomping, my brain locked up. I started to become frightened. I began to think and then *believed* they were going to kill me. But luckily, after years of self-preservation from all the hundreds of beatings from my mother, coupled with all the times I got picked on at school, I had learned to simply curl up into a ball and weather the storm. In the middle of my terror, the yelling, and the physical pain, there was an odd sense of peace. Suddenly the jolts of pain that shot through my body like volts of electricity weren't so shocking. *I can do this,* I told myself. *I can survive.*

I had always known for many, many years how meek and weak I appeared on the outside, for all to see and to tease and gawk at, but deep down inside I prided myself with a deep reserve that I could apply at will.

But then I did something stupid. Within a few seconds after the gang became tired of kick-the-geek aerobics and turned away, clapping their hands together in celebration, I became upset. I was mad at myself for always taking the hits—all those punches from the past, the endless stream of off-the-cuff remarks meant to stab me deep in the heart. I was sick and tired of lying on my side while others took pleasure in attacking me. Damn it, I screamed at myself, that was *my* boom box. My emotions got the better of me. I commanded myself to jump up. Then carefully and ever so quietly, with my heart pumping like a steam engine, I weaved my way into the middle of the group, and before anybody knew any better, I sprung up, snatched my radio, and blitzed away as fast as my feet and lungs could allow. My sole motivation was that if I got caught, I was so dead.

The next day I awoke to find a bruised body and a swollen red face. I was lucky. Damn lucky. My point: As awkward as it may seem, every once in a while all of us take a hit or two. Now, in the middle of your fear, you can try to do something physical, but that's not really the way to go, for even if you "win" that particular battle, you will take a lot more hits. And some blows can be fatal— whether physically, mentally, or spiritually. But in the middle of your situation, if you just focus and use your head, your chances of survival go up a gazillion percent. Get it?

When you find yourself curled up in your own ball of despair in the middle of your storm, I want you to center your thoughts, find a piece of calmness, and think your way out. **Fear does not have to be your enemy.** Just think, pull yourself up, and weave your way out of your difficulties. As a last resort—and I mean *last*—do what you need to do and run as fast as you can to get yourself away from your predicament.

Pardon the elementary school tone, but when you get scared: **Use your head.**

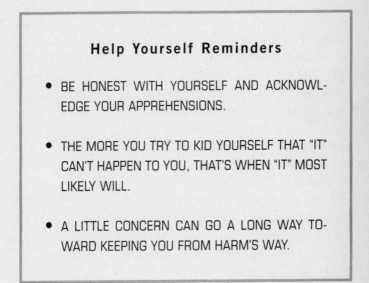

Help Yourself Reminders

- BE HONEST WITH YOURSELF AND ACKNOWL-EDGE YOUR APPREHENSIONS.

- THE MORE YOU TRY TO KID YOURSELF THAT "IT" CAN'T HAPPEN TO YOU, THAT'S WHEN "IT" MOST LIKELY WILL.

- A LITTLE CONCERN CAN GO A LONG WAY TO-WARD KEEPING YOU FROM HARM'S WAY.

Chapter 5

It's the F Word

Let's get right to it. There's something you should know. I can understand your embarrassment about this word, but at your age I strongly believe it's the most important word in your ever-expanding vernacular, meaning your vocabulary. Brace yourself. Here it is: the *F* word!

Come on, I know you're probably already thinking about it, and, quite frankly, I want you to. Think about it: The F word is an everyday part of life. Most people do it. And if everybody did, we'd have a lot fewer problems in the world. Heck, you wouldn't be here if it wasn't for it. In fact, when it comes to the F word, I want you to think about it in everything you do. At the very least I want you to think about it once an hour every day for the rest of your life.

Now, my publisher, their nervous attorneys, my agent, fellow colleagues, censors, and a league of other folks in the book industry have begged, pleaded, and even threatened to have me cast away on a deserted island—without the benefit of my daily dose of Starbucks triple espresso latte—if I stated the F word in this book. But I stood my ground. I fought for you. My argument was simple: If you're expected to act as a young adult, in which you carry yourself with responsibility, resilience, and with a sense of dignity, well, you're grown up enough to be admitted into the mature adults-only arena.

So, after much debate and gnashing of the teeth, I agreed, in part, that I wouldn't *say* the F word. But that doesn't mean I can't *spell out* some letters for you to decipher: F . . . U . . . C . . . You can figure out the rest. Now, for those of you who suffer from a spelling deficiency worse than me (seriously, I have extremely limited spelling skills; thank God for spell-checker and finding a bride who is a professional editor), the word I really mean to educate you on, that I want embedded in your skull for all time is: F . . . O . . . C . . . U . . . S. **Focus, focus, focus!**

Now I know you were smart enough to see through my little ruse, but if I got your blood to pump a little faster with anticipation and the hairs on the back of your neck to stand up in tingly excitement, good. Just as I want you to succeed, I also want to stimulate your thinking. That's the exact feeling you should have when your intensity is razor sharp. *That's* the feeling you should have when you're focused.

In the last chapter we went into detail about how to apply fear to your advantage. How do you do that? Focus. You concentrate your intensity on what is vital to you in that particular situation. Some of you may say, "Man, I can't ever seem to focus on anything. My mind's all over the place. I never can concentrate for more than a second at a time." Well, that's not true. When you pick out clothes to wear, choose what you want to eat, or make dozens if not hundreds of decisions daily, you are in fact concentrating on what is important to you for *that particular sit-*

uation at that time. So give yourself some credit. If you lack a certain focus, simply 1) slow down, 2) gather your thoughts, and 3) apply yourself a little more. If you can consciously give thought to the everyday things (which you already do), then take your focus to the next level on the more vital elements of your life.

Now I can give you a wordy, lengthy example on how the brain operates, but basically when there's some tension, when there's something that becomes important to you—whether it's that car you long for or that person who's so dreamy—these longings have a tendency to dominate your thoughts *and* push other elements aside.

Especially when it comes to extremely serious circumstances, as on September 11. What mattered? Did all those tests you had to take or the seemingly overwhelming problems you had with your parents or others close to you? On a more personal side, what about the trouble you had with your hair or the status of your clothes? Or what about what others may have thought of you at that time? With all that was happening that day in September, did any of those things truly matter? I sincerely doubt it.

Focus Puts Everything into Perspective

Have you discovered that you have the capacity to concentrate in times of duress or in truly horrible of situations? If so, why? Because at that time nothing else matters. There's nothing to distract you. So much is at stake. You become conscious of the smallest details. You're scared. You don't wish for anything bad to happen.

And that's good. As I've said before, be a little apprehensive about the possible outcome—on how you act, how you apply yourself, what you say, what you think, how you react with others. And in some cases that same concern keeps you away from disastrous predicaments that could haunt you for the rest of your life.

Think about it. Use your head, stay focused, and stay out of trouble.

So what helped save me that afternoon alone with my deranged mother? You guessed it: the ability to focus. Let's look at that situation a little deeper.

My entire being became focused on the singular thought of burning to death. The more I stared at the flames, the more I could visualize my fate. Even the pulsating pain from my right arm seemed to fade away. I took a deep breath. While avoiding Mother's frame, my eyes darted in every other direction. For no reason my ears caught the clicking sound of the hands on the electric clock that hung above the doorway. In my excited state I drew in another breath while staring at the clock that read 3:50 in the afternoon. I repeated the time over and over: "Ten minutes till four o'clock. Ten minutes till four . . ."

Suddenly it came to me. *"Time!"* my brain screamed. My two brothers come home from their Boy Scout meeting precisely at four o'clock, and Mother never acts this bizarre in front of them or my father. So if I can just slow her down, if I can beg, borrow, steal, and buy just ten minutes' worth of time, then maybe today I won't die!

In the heat of the moment those words, *then maybe today I won't die,* made all the years of defeating self-doubt and the load of shame I carried on my shoulders for more than four years seem to evaporate, and a river of tears began to flow. Doing whatever I could so I didn't end up on top of the gas stove, burning like a piece of meat, was the only thing that mattered. Just the idea of a chance of dying forced me to focus.

No lies. No dramatics. I'm telling it to you straight. Being focused saved my life.

So how did I do it? How did I steal ten minutes' worth of time? Simple. I did so one second at a time. I was able to use everything that for years was a form of twisted punishment and flipped it around to my advantage.

"Did you hear me?" Mother yelled. "Quit your sniveling. Get your carcass up from the kitchen floor and lay down on the gas stove! Move it, you . . . you piece of filth!" she finished with an extra burst of hatred.

But suddenly none of that mattered. Her words that had crushed me before now meant nothing to me, just unpleasant sounds spewing from the hole in her mouth. Big deal. If anything, I wanted her to berate me as much as she willed, until she turned blue in the face and passed out.

With some of her energy expended, Mother huffed above me with her hands on her hips. She took a few short breaths before snapping her head in the direction of her drink. She began to reach out before taking a few steps forward to reach for her prize. That's when I knew I had a chance.

She swirled the contents of the drink in her hand. Took a sip. Swallowed. Closed her eyes as if to feel the rush. Opened them. Adjusted her blurred vision at me still on the floor. Roared at me again, commanding me to stand up. Snapped her fingers as a sign of enforcement.

All I could think was *Tick-Tock, Tick-Tock*.

For years whenever Mother clicked her fingers, it meant I had but a single second to snap to the "position of address"—stand exactly three feet in front of her with my chin glued to my chest, eyes locked on the floor, and my hands glued to my sides. I wasn't to breathe or move a single muscle unless granted permission to do so. Any deviation—a blink of my eyes or a wobble from my weak knees—constituted a crime which would instantly unleash hell's fury.

For years I obeyed, yet still hell followed. So now I "obeyed" but by my own set of rules. I stood up . . . but I took two extra seconds. I stood in front of her . . . but slid my feet a few inches back. My hands were on the side of my legs . . . but because of the injury to my right arm, I could not get it to remain still and finally cradled it with my left one.

This, of course, drove Mother crazy, and she unleashed another string of obscenities that I heard a million times; it sapped away more of her energy and forced her to soothe her nerves with yet another drink. *Tick-Tock*.

I sensed an opportunity. I dared committing the ultimate sin. Without permission I slowly scanned the length of her body until my eyes met hers, and I whimpered, "Wha . . . wha . . . wha . . . di . . . did . . . I . . . d . . . do . . . wro . . . wrong?"

Mother nearly blew a gasket. First her mouth almost hit the floor, then her shock made her stutter as she asked, ***"What did you say?"***

Well, since she asked a question, I *had* to answer by repeating my original question, but this time only slower—which forced her to become spellbound yet again and take another drink before "coming to her senses" and punching me in the face.

I took the hit. I didn't mind a bit. I've had worse. With blood seeping from my nose and dripping from the side of my mouth, my motivation was the hissing sound of the burning gas from the stove and the bluish purple flames. My reward was watching the black hand from the kitchen clock crawl its way toward the appointed time.

The cycle continued. Mother would hit me, I'd fall to the floor, struggle to stand up, slide my feet as far back as I dared, never quite able to maintain my rigid "position of address" but instead constantly fidget in front of her, stuttering out words that made no sense in my "delusional" state, forcing Mother to repeat the cycle between her expletive nouns and never-ending amounts of alcohol over and over and over again.

As I write these words to you, now looking back at that afternoon, I can honestly state that as sensational as that scene may seem, the plan itself was basically simple. If you really think about it, all of us take a few hits in our life—whether physically, psychologically, spiritually, or financially—in love, at work, or at school. All of us receive an unexpected blow or two. And it hurts. It's not fair. It's only in finding that inner strength to brush yourself off, stand up, and truly gain something positive from the predicament that truly matters. **That's** the mark of a true adult. **That's** someone I hold in the highest esteem.

And that's what I want and quite frankly expect from you. Take life's unexpected punches, no matter how wrong or upsetting they may be, clean yourself off, stand tall, and make your life all the better because of it!

Because of my fear of the possible outcome, I was able to maintain an intense focus. I also had a little bit of luck: My older brother, Ron, came home a few minutes early from his Boy Scout meeting. To this day Ron, who has been a police officer for more than twenty years now and, God bless him, saves children from similar circumstances, has no idea how much of a role he played for me that day. For the first time I was able to physically, spiritually, and psychologically stand up for myself. As previously stated, I was neither brave nor extraordinary in any way, shape, or form. I couldn't quit, and the situation forced me to rely on myself. Basically, I simply did what I had to do.

And I am no different from the millions upon millions of others who truly gave their all when it mattered.

Sacrifice for a Higher Cause

As you grow in years and fully mature as an adult, you will truly comprehend the wonder of America and all that it has achieved in its grand experiment of democracy. America was founded on the sole premise of individual freedom. And through that pursuit our founding fathers, mothers, sons, and daughters took a few hits. In fact, a lot of them. Yet they stood up for their beliefs, made sacrifices, and suffered, and many of them paid the ultimate price for their dreams. Yet the intensity of their drive never wavered. The more they suffered, the harder it became, and the more they maintained their will to prevail.

America is one of the only nations in the world where ordinary people can fulfill extraordinary dreams. And with every great feat comes enormous adversity. When most of the nation woke up early one Sunday morning, they discovered we were in a state of war. Many debated whether America stood a chance of winning World War II. Some scholars debated it could take anywhere from fifteen to eighteen years. Think of it: fifteen years of gas rationing, limited food, possibly sleeping in subway tunnels while homes and neighborhoods are bombed to rubble, and men, women, *and* children working for the cause. For *fifteen years.* The Allied Forces, knowing full well the magnitude of our country's annihilation if we failed, made their determination all the more. Brave men, women, and even children at that time, whose depth and appreciation can never be repaid, fought against overwhelming odds and defeated two separate nations on both sides of the globe in less than four years.

Years ago, President John F. Kennedy challenged the country with landing a man on the moon within the span of a decade even though at the time the Soviet Union seemingly surpassed the United States by having already successfully launched the world's first satellite *and* the world's first man into space. At the time, our nation's rockets were dangerously unreliable, exploding after takeoff or even on the launchpad itself. But as the great Greek philosopher Archimedes once said, "Give me a lever long enough, and I'll move the world." After many sacrifices, including those who perished, an estimated 100,000 individuals, in their pursuit of the unimaginable, in just a few years made the seemingly impossible possible. As the great *Apollo 11* astronaut Neil Armstrong humbly spoke from the surface of the lunar planet, "One small step for man; one giant leap for mankind." Immortal words that could have been stated by extraordinary individuals before and after that place in time in any and all situations. Simple raw determination drives individuals to achieve their greatness. And the more the setbacks, the more that defeatable chances only propel those who are truly focused all the more.

In my many years of travels, I have been fortunate enough to meet literally millions of folks—those who overcame near-death, those who seemingly never had a chance at the slightest prospect of success, those who were raised in the most despicable of upbringings. The one thing they **all** have deep within their heart is the unconquerable drive to prevail, an indomitable human spirit.

This is why I have the highest respect for those like McKayla Hanson. Not only did she endure a private hell of extreme child abuse, but at age seven, doctors were convinced that she was going to die due to rhabdomyosarcoma, a type of cancer that affects the bones. Hanson lost her right leg as well as part of her pelvic and hip bone to the terminal disease. Fighting for her life, McKayla did so with the support of her newly adoptive family. Even while scared and losing her hair, Hanson found something along the way: **herself.** To quote this brave young lady: "I had to be strong."

Now if anyone had the right to cry about how unfair life can be or to say she wanted to cave in and give up, it would be McKayla. After enduring two years of extensive radiation and chemotherapy *and* more surgeries, she simply kept going. With her cancer now in remission, this young teenager is not only walking with the aid of a prosthetic leg but runs and swims with one leg. And from what I hear, Miss Hanson does quite well. In her first track meet she came in fourth . . . out of seven! "I was scared and I cried. But I did it." McKayla, who never had any interest in sports before cancer, now says through her self-determination, "I wouldn't be as brave."

That is the one thing that makes McKayla and those you admire and respect great, even phenomenal. It is what will separate you from others who whine, don't care, who don't even *wish* to better themselves. It's the ability to focus on what is truly important—no matter how many roadblocks, setbacks, limitations, or "hits" you endure. In the end what carries you through is the focused determination to want **it** more!

So how bad do you want **it?** How bad do you want to receive good grades, graduate college, and live a full, rich life? How bad do you want to purchase that car, date that boy, or go out with that girl? What are you willing to do and how much are you willing to sacrifice in order to achieve *your* desires?

It's All About You

I want you to succeed, but you and you alone have to be willing to carry the load. Your parents, relatives, guardians, teachers, coaches, neighbors, and friends—God love 'em and bless 'em—can only help you so far.

These are the thoughts of legendary L.A. Lakers basketball coach Phil Jackson, who not only has a championship ring from when he played professional basketball but has eight others for leading the Chicago Bulls to impressive victories before doing the same for the Lakers. A fellow coach says of Jackson, "Most coaches call time-outs and kind of let the players rely on the coach. In Phil's case I think he kind of says, 'You have to rely on yourself, because when it comes to crunch time, I'm not out there on the floor with you. I can only do so many things.' "

Remember these words: When it comes to your own "crunch time," your parents, relatives, guardians, teachers, coaches, neighbors, friends, or whoever won't be "out there" with you! They can only do so many things. So the sooner you learn to focus on becoming self-reliant, the better.

Live it, love it, and learn it. Get in the habit of telling yourself, "If it's to be, it's up to me!"

You want something? Good for you. Dig deep down within yourself. Push yourself further than you ever thought possible. Bit by bit, day by day, strive to achieve your greatness. Be consistent every day on the small things (more on that later). Filter out the negative junk and maintain your focus. Apply this formula now at your age, and you will be ahead of others twice your age in a very short period of time.

You make it happen.

When there's something important, something that truly matters, keep in mind it's not going to happen overnight. No way. No matter what others may excitedly claim, the reality of life is different. That's the truth. And I think that's a good thing. Why? When you land your dream, achieve that goal that only you thought possible, you'll know in your heart *you* did it. No silver spoon, no daddy's little girl, no Mr. Popular who seemingly just shows up and *wham* gets everything. Just you and your raw determination. So, okay, you may miss out on a few social events, which in a matter of weeks, days, or even hours are forgotten for what they were—a letdown, a waste of time, nothing. And you may have to study late into the night just to hang on to your grade point average. Then, on top of everything, you may have to stand outside in the freezing rain all night for a mere chance at . . . But, hey, if that's what it takes, you have my respect. I say "good on you." Just stay focused!

One of the most trying, frustrating times for me as a young man was when I had to fight, scramble, and humble myself with every ounce I had just to serve in the military. At the time, it seemed as if everyone else waltzed in and signed up for adventures aboard while serving their country, and I was treated like the plague. Truth be told, I brought part of it upon myself: bad decisions and not pursuing my education so I could work myself to death more than ninety hours a week as a freshman in high school for $1.65 an hour. And part of it was bad luck—being a day late, the wrong form filed at the wrong office with the wrong person, off-the-wall, unexplainable accidents hours before my medical examination. Whatever. Bottom line: The United States Air Force didn't want anything to do with me. I was a high school dropout who asininely believed: "*I* don't need no schoolin' to make it out there. I'm never gonna need to understand math, English, social sciences, or whatever else to make it in the real world. All I need is a strong back to make it out there." Duh!

Now, in my defense, I slaved away and threw away my education because I was engulfed with the terror of being broke and homeless when I "aged out" of foster care. And as much as I thought I was trying to impress those hard-nosed air force recruiters with my strong work ethic, they were anything but impressed. All they saw was a scrawny eighteen-year-old kid who was scared of his own shadow. When addressed or even asked the simplest of questions, I'd duck my head toward the floor and stutter for minutes at a time, knowing full well what a complete jerk I was making of myself. If that weren't enough, my "I don't need no schoolin', 'cause I'll never use such and such in the real world" bit me in the behind like a coiled rattlesnake when I failed to make the lowest of scores on the military academics achievement test. But for me the worst sin was when one of the sergeants scowled at me after he found out I was a foster child. "So, tell me, boy, what'd you do to land yourself in foster care? You got a problem with authority? Well, do ya, boy?" To say I was crushed, humbled, and humiliated was a vast understatement.

To say the least, I knew it was going to be a struggle. After running to my foster home, slamming shut my door to the world, and crying in my bed about how unfair everything was, I calmed down, cleared my head, and *then* applied my thoughts to my advantage. All I had to do, I instructed myself, was tap into my secret weapon. I knew in my heart that if I could endure all that I had as a kid in Mother's house for all those years, then I could buck up, suck it up, and endure whatever it took so I could enlist. I adopted the singular mind-set that I would do whatever I had to do to make my goal happen. My focus every day, every morning, was that nothing in the world would stop me from achieving my objective.

I admit at times it sucked. Before work, after work, rain, shine, cold or foggy weather, I made it a point to show up nearly every day on the front steps of the recruiter's office before they opened. I made it a point to study every brochure, scrutinize every video on every job the air force offered, and I began to understand the basics of military protocol and customs. I let it be known that I took over and over again every division of every military scholastic test until *I* was satisfied with the scores, which in some cases were beyond the air force's acceptance level. In between working sixty to eighty hours a week at the time and loitering at the recruiter's station, after numerous frustrating and humiliating attempts I finally received my G.E.D. Overall it took me six months—six months of enduring a self-degrading and embarrassing whirlwind of emotions. **But** when I finally stood up, raised my hand, and pledged to serve my country, every fiber of my being swelled with pride—immense pride that I still carry to this very day.

Was it worth it? You bet. I can never put into words the sense of honor and dignity I carry with me, especially now at my age. Not only was the air force my surrogate family that gave me, taught me so much, but it allowed me the privilege of serving my country, of providing a grain of sand in a moment of history, while living the adventure of a lifetime!

Bottom line: Even with a few lucky breaks and all those seemingly endless roadblocks, the truth is that it was my resolve that saw me through. All I had to do was chip away a little here, a little there, day after day after day, until I could catch a glimmer of light at the end of the tunnel that led to my goal. It was focus. And it will be *your* focus that will make everything fall into place.

All you have to do is maintain your vision. Just sustain your drive.

This is one of the main reasons that I'm writing this book, especially if you have experienced a few hard knocks. And if you have, you have my sympathies and respect, but that will only get you so far. I've found that for the most part young adults do "want it" more. You're more than willing to see it through. In fact, did you know that your youth, your stamina, your inner drive far exceeds that of those my age? *And . . .*

Life Gets Old

I'm not out to run anyone down, particularly generations older than yours, but I've found that it's hard to keep adults inspired. Oh, sure, some buy the latest Change Your Life in One Day or Less video, DVD, or CD. Some go off for a well-deserved motivational weekend where they get fired up, clap till their hands fall off, and laugh, cry, dance, and hug, hug, hug. Or for the ultimate climax—for those willing to tap into their inner inner child's child that they lost, neglected, or never nurtured in the first place (once again we stumble onto unresolved issues): to walk on coals. If that works for some folks, then more power to ya. I give kudos to anyone who truly strives to better themselves. However, nine times out of ten when one returns home and goes back to the drudgery of work, and the realities of life soon take over, all that hoopla quickly fades.

Why? Because the older we get, the harder it is to *want* to change. We've become complacent, settled in *our* ways. It's easier to stick with old habits than to constantly strive, day in and day out, for something that we believe in the back of our minds, mainly because of past failures, we may not be able to achieve anyway. So, many folks figure: Why even bother?

That's why you may have seen a fair amount of adults who at the time had the best of intentions to go on that diet, finish that project, visit that place they've dreamt about since they were a child, or finally do "that thing" they've talked about forever. But a majority of the time, through absolutely no fault of their own, something happens. Life happens. Someone becomes sick or is laid off from work; the car breaks down; little Joey needs braces; expenses skyrocket; or one becomes mired in internal family matters. Maybe there was a fire, a tornado, an earthquake, or a flood. The list can be endless. As you are well aware, in life anything and everything can happen.

If that weren't enough, add to the equation that the older we get, the more conservative we become. Folks don't want to lose what they've worked so hard for all their lives.

Let's slow down and repeat that sentence again, but this time I want you to say it out loud slowly: "Folks don't want to lose what *they've* worked so hard for all *their* lives." Part of that is safeguarding our most cherished assets: our families, mainly our children. Almost all parents struggle to find that balance (which no parent has yet to achieve) of protecting their children from the atrocities of the world while training their children—as they become older, in their preteen years—to make competent decisions when they step out into the world. Many parents, myself included, do our damnedest, with limited success, to make sure our children don't repeat the same asinine, if not near fatal, mistakes we made at—you guessed it— *your* age. Might this be one of the reasons that your

parents crack down on you and want you to remain focused at this stage of your life? All in all, is that really such
a horrible thing?

Comedian and film star Bernie Mac was raised by his
grandmother after his mother passed away when he was a
young teen. He gives much credit to the ladies who kept
young Bernie constantly in line in the midst of a tough
neighborhood. Some of the lessons he learned he now
passes on to others: "Suffering is a good teacher. It keeps
you in its grip until you've learned your lesson." "If you
mess something up, remember who got you there. The
only one you got to blame is yourself." "Sometimes when
you lose, you win. Failure is just life's way of preparing you
for success." And "You have to meet all of the challenges,
big and small. Because how you start is how you finish."

Then, besides how adults raise their children, there are
other assets such as their homes, their cars, their life savings, their whatevers that, again, *they've* sacrificed and
worked so hard for long *before* you were even conceived.

Now you may huff and puff and roll your eyes and say
to yourself, "It's no big deal. My folks don't work that
hard." Really? Maybe, maybe not. Maybe not *now,* but a
lot of adults have **so** paid their dues just so you can live
the life that you do today. Especially those single moms
and dads and individuals like Tom Cruise and Bernie Mac,
as well as scores of others who fought for equality in the
workforce, as well as everyone else who just a short time
ago were darn lucky *if* they received $1.65 an hour for
their minimum wage.

With all due respect, who are *you* to judge *them?*

And speaking quite frankly, the older one gets, the
more relaxed one becomes. A lot of folks would rather or-

der something off the Internet than jump in their car and drive around town in traffic all morning, just to wait in line for a half hour to pick up a few items. And on the more lackadaisical side, for whatever their reasoning, there are folks who spend more time and effort looking for that guaranteed, instantaneous "quick fix" remedy to all their problems rather than apply themselves little by little, rain or shine.

Some folks simply feel too worn down to go "out there" and "go for it," to push it to the extreme anymore. Hell, they're tired! Working full-time, running a house, doing everyday stuff, putting out everyday fires (problems), and being a parent can kill a person. Some can't stay up to watch the *Late Show with David Letterman*, let alone catch the ten o'clock news. Heck, I'm over the hill myself, in my midforties, and can no longer run fifteen miles at a stretch, work more than eighteen hours a day, six days a week, or survive with three hours of sleep a night. I simply can't do it anymore. I now have to be a better manager of my time, get more rest, and be very careful of my health—especially when indulging on that chocolate cheesecake that's sitting on the kitchen table taunting me. *Umm, chocolate.*

Nowadays a phenomenal day for me is when I'm home—which is still rare. After returning from my morning workout, which now consists of more cardio (because I have a small cheesecake addiction) than free weights, I love nothing more than to walk my three adorable spoiled-rotten dogs, take my time reading the paper, sip my freshly brewed cup of coffee with sugar replacement, chat with my wife, and listen to jazz. Besides my recent addiction to golf, *this* is living large.

And remember, this is coming from a man who used to jump out of airplanes and fly all over the globe on adventurous classified missions for the U.S. Air Force while working part-time in juvenile hall between flights, spending every second I could with my son, and charting any "free time" traveling up and down the entire state of California to assist others with their issues.

But now sometimes, as I sit outside staring at the purple-red skyline, watching the sun disappear over the jagged mountain peaks, I count my blessings and I feel my age. And sometimes uneasiness creeps up on me as a persistent voice cries, "Dave, what happened to you? Walking dogs, sitting down, sitting still, reading the paper, drinking coffee, chasing a stupid white ball. And *you* call this fun? What in the hell happened?

Now don't get me wrong. I have and always will continue to push and better myself, work hard, and learn as much as I can with each passing day, *but* as the gritty film character Inspector Harry Callahan of the famed *Dirty Harry* series stated many times, "Man's got to know his limitations."

Life happens! And sooner than you realize, all of this will happen to you. Trust me, you're going to take a nap and wake up in your midthirties, with thinning hair, love handles around your once-trim slender waist, and wondering where life went. A few naps later, people will think you're impatient, constantly complaining, and you need to rest, and you're going to think to yourself, What's wrong with them? Wake up from one more nap, and you discover your mind is slipping and parts of your body that you were once so proud of have become an embarrassment, sagging south. Then the enviable question all of us ask is: "How did I get here? What happened? If I only did a little more, tried a little harder." Then your ears will ring with: "Darn it. If I was only a little bit more focused on what was truly important and wanted it more, then maybe, just maybe, I could have lived a little bit more, been a little happier."

Remember that line I gave you from chapter one: "To **live.** Now **that** would be an adventure!"

I hope I'm not confusing you, for my concern is simply this: At this stage in your life you have to stay focused, work hard, be willing to sacrifice when needed, and want it, crave it, and desire it more every single day for many, many years, so that when life happens, *when* tragedies strike, *when* age creeps up on you, you will already have that strong foundation to stand on and possess those building blocks on which you can build further. Because there is no escaping it, life will happen.

Now you may be saying to yourself, "Wow, this is way too intense! It's a whole lot more than I bargained for. I wasn't expecting all of *this!*" You're right. You are absolutely correct. This is a whole lot more, but then again, this is my job——to help prepare you for all this.

And, yes, I freely admit I have been rather firm with you. Never forget that part of my job is to challenge you, to help propel you to the next level in your life. For as challenging as your life may already have been, as difficult as you think the outside world may be, it **is** a hundred times more grueling than you can imagine. I'm not saying it's bad out there. Believe me, if anything it's a wonderful venture. It's just the more you can work on yourself now, the more prepared you will be for your future.

As you know, it's not all milk and cookies. And at times it is hard to crawl out of bed and fight the good fight day after day. This is why I applaud you for at least going this far. This is why I choose to work with you, especially if you have not had the best upbringing or maybe have made a few mistakes. That's okay. A person who strives to do better, to right a wrong, shows a lot of guts and courage. This is why you need to develop these responsible habits now.

I'm sure you've been around the block enough to understand there are a lot of folks who, for whatever reason or excuse, cannot (or refuse to) do anything to get themselves out of whatever hole they fell into—unless, of course, someone picks them up and carries them around in their customized backpack. And for lack of better verbiage, there are a fair amount of young adults who are spoiled stupid. That no matter what, someone will always be there for them all day for the rest of their days.

Piece of advice: Let those folks do their own thing, find their own way. Don't waste a moment of your energy or valuable time on them. Let them live their life as you begin yours. Sooner or later they will learn their lesson. Life has a way of doing that. Life happens. Just stay focused on *you*.

What's Driving You?

If you've fallen behind in school, had some trouble at home or work, had to push yourself a little harder to make the sports team, then I say *good for you!* In more wise words from Bernie Mac, "If you want a helping hand, look at the end of your arm." In other words, *you've* earned it.

Sometimes the worst things that can happen to you or against you can be extremely motivational, positive, life-altering experiences. Why? They teach us all that life is not perfect. When you're slapped down and hate how that feels, you make darn sure it never happens again. How? You concentrate on not allowing yourself to be in that position again. Period. You focus on what truly matters in improving your life for the better: getting good grades, getting along with others, concentrating on every play of every game—how you act and what you say. Make it a part of your everyday lifestyle. **Focus, focus, focus.**

Under some circumstances when push comes to shove, you have to focus on what's imperative; you have to dig down deep within yourself and, above all, you have to want it more. Every day when I read the paper I come across stories that are utterly amazing: A man survives alone in the wilderness with nothing but a compass, a small knife, common sense, and willpower. A person on the brink of death reaches full recovery. A single mom who dropped out of high school to raise three kids works two full-time jobs and eventually earns a college degree with honors. Wow!

You've heard the stories, read the magazines, and seen these epics in the movies. What every one of these folks has *is* an indomitable human spirit. That deep inner drive to overcome, to better themselves no matter their past, no matter how many times they've been slapped down, stepped on, or kicked around. Their drive to succeed far outweighs anything negative they've experienced. They're focused. And, *ta-da,* they simply wanted it more.

Like Erik Weihenmayer, blind since he was thirteen. As a thirty-three-year-old he climbed to the top of famed twenty-nine-thousand-foot Mount Everest. Now keep in mind, 90 percent of climbers fail to reach the summit, and many die trying. And by the way, how high is twenty-nine thousand feet? I used to midair-refuel aircraft as low as ten thousand feet and as high as twenty-five thousand feet!

And while Mr. Weihenmayer had some support, he still accomplished his dream on his own. He did it while he was sick, dehydrated, and bloodied—and that was just the first floor of the tallest mountain in the world, the "lower" camp one, which Erik stumbled into literally green in the face. A teammate and fellow climber said, "He looked like prizefighter George Foreman had beat him up for two hours." Not just another yuppie adventurist, Weihenmayer began applying himself to mountaineering at age twenty. With all climbs, especially the unforgiving, constantly ice-shifting Everest, one mistake, one small misstep, and Erik and those around him could fall off the "edge of the world" or into a one-thousand-plus-foot crevasse.

So how did he do it? As simple as this sounds, Mr. Weihenmayer accomplished his task by focusing step by step on everything, and I do mean on every single thing he *did* or *did not* do.

Erik, who has a wife and baby girl, says, "There are summits everywhere. You just have to know where to look."

I've said it before and I'll say it again: Nothing can conquer or dominate the human spirit. One only has to harness one's ambitions.

That afternoon when my mother tried to have me submit and lay down on that gas stove, I began a lifelong journey of intense focusing that I maintain to this day; it's a part of my everyday lifestyle. Just like brushing my teeth or getting dressed. I concentrate on how to achieve my goals for that particular day.

In some awkward sense, that situation and others to follow were perhaps the most positive experiences of my life. My past gave me a deep sense of pride that I never thought I had; it took me beyond what I thought I was capable of achieving and made me strong. And the same can be true for you!

It's All You

Another hard truth I'm going to give you is that in life don't *expect* anything from anybody. Period. Never demand let alone expect anything that you can do yourself for yourself. I fully realize that statement may upset a few people who foolishly, if not stupidly, believe that "someone" will always be there for them, that "someone" owes them "something" or that the "system" will and/or must provide for them, or that "the man" is keeping them down.

That's a bunch of cow patties. *If* it were true, exactly how far did "these" folks go in their lives? What exactly did *they* accomplish? Or did they develop the habit of focusing on a lifetime of nonstop excuses? *So-and-so did me wrong . . . if it wasn't for such and such, I would have, could have . . . I tell you what, one of these days I'm gonna . . .* Hmm, as I asked before, are these people who believe in such nonsense and such statements a success? Are they happy? Are they a success? Hmm?

Another thought to keep in mind is when push came to

shove, did these same folks really, truly give it all that they had to better themselves? Did they possess that craving to accomplish something extraordinary against the odds? *Or,* before the going got tough, did they develop the mantra "Wow, this is way too much for me. I . . . I ah . . . quit"?

To be fair, I admit that nine times out of ten something did happen in their lives, ***but*** all in all, everyone—and I mean ***everyone—is* responsible** for the outcome of their own life. Not Mom, Dad, Grandma, Grandpa, that teacher, or that hard-nosed coach. It doesn't amount to a hill of beans if you were raised in a country club–like neighborhood, the suburbs, the barrio, or the worst ghetto on the planet. Skin color, religious preference, gay, straight, short, tall, skinny, chunky, four eyes, **whatever,** it's up to you!

I know you've been exposed to folks who think or believe someone is holding them back or keeping them down. Use your head. Ask yourself: Where do you see that person or that group in three, five, ten years? Are they truly going to become something let alone graduate high school?

Please, please, please don't be taken in by that junk. You know better, so do better. If anything, devour those stories of that single mom who did it all, that medical miracle person who defied all odds, or that lost soul who never gave up and walked out of that circumstance all the better for it. These people, these stories, will help to educate, inspire, and expand your horizons when it comes to maintaining *your* focus and *your* drive to better *yourself.*

Help Yourself Reminders

- YOU'RE OLD ENOUGH AND WISE ENOUGH TO UNDERSTAND AND IMPLEMENT THE TRUE MEANING OF THE *F* WORD.

- UNDERSTAND AND APPRECIATE WHAT OTHERS HAVE ACCOMPLISHED IN ORDER TO MAKE YOUR LIFE BETTER.

- REALIZE THAT OTHERS CAN ONLY HELP YOU SO MUCH.

- LIFE GOES BY QUICKLY, SO BUILD THAT SOLID FOUNDATION FOR YOURSELF NOW BEFORE *LIFE HAPPENS* TO YOU!

- DISCOVER THAT INNER DRIVE AND NEVER, NEVER GIVE IT UP OR TOSS IT AWAY WHEN THINGS GET A LITTLE ROUGH.

- UNDERSTAND THAT NO ONE AND NOTHING PREVENTS *YOU* FROM ACHIEVING YOUR AMBITIONS. YOU JUST HAVE TO FOCUS ON *YOUR* CAUSE AND BE WILLING TO *WANT* IT MORE.

Part Two

CHOICES YOU MAKE NOW AND WHERE THEY CAN LEAD YOU IN YOUR FUTURE

Chapter 6

Your Life, Your Choice

How is it that some folks "make it" while others do not? That some folks constantly accomplish extraordinary feats while others can't even obtain mediocrity? In part it could be unresolved issues that keep pulling folks backward. Maybe they feel defeated, have little or no concern for what's going on around them, or maybe they lack the drive and simply aren't focused. Or it could be a combination of all these and more.

With all the preceding possible elements, the one primary factor is **it was their decision.** It was their decision to address **or** not address those issues, to allow **or** not allow themselves to become discouraged, to have regard for what may happen to them, **or** to concentrate and push themselves to accomplish their goals. In one way or another, all of us decide what we are **and** what are not willing to do. Whether it is cleaning the room now, putting off that homework till later, coming to terms with those issues, or staying mad at the world, the choice is basically ours.

Simply put, the life you lead now and the life you live in the near future **will** be based largely on what **you** decide.

Again, if you can get out of bed, pick out your clothes,

and choose what you want to eat for breakfast, well, to me, you can obviously *choose* for yourself. If you stay in bed all day, go to school naked, or do not have the proper nutrients in your body that you need to stay sharp and fit, you will have to deal with those consequences.

You, you, you, **you.**

Have you ever heard others your age who always state with all the bitterness they can that it's not "them" but someone or something else? "It ain't my fault. I didn't do anything. Teacher so-and-so made me fail." Really? Well, then, whose responsibility was it? What did or didn't they do? Exactly how does anyone, let alone a teacher who wants nothing more than to advance others through education, prevent someone from achievement?

That same group of embittered young adults who find themselves in serious trouble almost always proclaim for all the world to hear: "It was my parents. . . . School sucks. . . . I had to drop out. . . . I had a bad childhood. . . . It's society's fault. . . . I'm a victim. . . ."

Whatever! The list can go on and on. But know this: Usually once the "excuse habit" is formed and the older one becomes, it's terribly hard to break the cycle.

To be fair, there is some truth to adjusting to a broken marriage, troubles in the classroom, a dysfunctional if not violent childhood, or living within a community that is filled with overwhelming prejudice and limited nurturing opportunities.

I respect that and more. I truly do. And you have my deepest sympathies. But my ounce or two of pity won't even get you a cup of coffee. Receiving the compassion from others is nice, but, speaking quite frankly, if you want my respect and that of others around you, then make the decision to turn things around for the better by improving your situation, your attitude, and thus your life.

Your Fate You Make

Unless someone is attached to you all day and night with a gun to your head telling you how to dress, walk, talk, what to study or not study in school, who to hang out with, how you should act, or—more extreme—to join a gang, then breaking the law, promoting terror, or finding that "high" to "escape" all your problems while at the same time killing yourself on drugs, well, then, it is/was **your decision**.

So, if you want to act "all that" and do all those things, at least be man enough or woman enough to take responsibility for the decisions *you've* made! Out of your own self-respect, whatever happens, good or bad, be an adult and take accountability for your life rather than run down the endless list of BS excuses.

Choose Wisely

Where can decisions lead you? Come on, you know the answer. As much as I push for you to be the sole person behind your success, with just a fair amount of focus and basic determination you *will* go far in life, especially when compared to others around you who are stuck in their endless "victim" routine or self-destructive behaviors. Bottom line: Just as those determined young children later became NASA's finest, venturing into the far reaches of space, it is you and you alone who must decide just how far you wish to journey.

On the opposite end of that scale, thoughtless, lack-adaisical, unconcerned decisions, or those that become deliberately defiant, will lead you—if not now, then later—to absolute despair. Period. There is no other way to state this. If you go around making those types of decisions, you're only screwing yourself. Once again I pose the question: Aren't you better than that? And don't you deserve better?

If you're in the habit of making bad choices, don't try to convince yourself: "Well things aren't *that* bad. I can make up for it sometime later." And while those statements are basically true, that tomorrow is another day, another day to begin anew and/or to redeem one's self, I wouldn't bet my life, my happiness on second, third, fourth, fifth, or however many chances are needed to re-deem one's self.

Case in point: Years ago when I worked in juvenile hall, I learned that because of the severity of some of the minors' crimes, some were to be transferred from our fa-cility to a "more secure" institution. Sometimes a supervi-sor and I were given the task of transporting the tough youngster, who while at juvenile hall acted "all that." The attitude was "I'm so tough. I'm so bad, so cool. No one's gonna tell me what to do. I don't need anyone or any-thing. I can kick anybody's ass."

It didn't take a rocket scientist to understand that once someone got to know most of these young adults, they were basically the same as the millions of other teens across America. They laughed, they cried, they were con-fused, frustrated, and a little lost. They loved movies, cars, clothes, the opposite sex, yadda yadda. Again, no major difference. Now, a lot of folks might think they all came from broken homes, impoverished backgrounds, or pasts so dark and so horrible that one would obviously understand how they ended up where they did.

Well, that's not necessary true. My first "intake" was a young, bubbly, naive, shaggy-haired teen named Jamie who was initially busted for petty theft. One afternoon Jamie got mad at his folks who couldn't afford that "thing" Jamie craved. His attitude was that he desired "it," so he stole "it," was caught, arrested, and began to despise his parents more because he "wouldn't be at 'the Hall' if they had only got him that thing." This began a process of adopting new friends "who understood," losing all interest in school, which of course led to revolving in and out of juvenile hall and more increasing crimes, which ultimately led to the cycle of hating his parents and school and becoming more drawn to his angered friends.

After returning from flying overseas for many months for the air force, on my first shift back I discovered that Jamie, who initially was just a mixed-up kid, was being transported that day to the California Youth Authority, which is basically a prison for teens. In part because of the time that had passed, I could barely recognize Jamie. He had grown so tall, but more so his demeanor, his entire attitude had changed—he shuffled his feet, the way he kept his hair covering his once-bright eyes, his tone of voice was different, and he used profanity for every other word he uttered. This was not the agreeable everyday teen I had known just a short time ago. The only element of Jamie that shone through his "all that" tough-guy act was his laugh, but that even had a coldness to it.

His "all that" act of being so mean, so bad, so cool, "I'm gonna kick the world's butt" attitude was so dead-on,

I would have given him an Oscar for best actor. Even as my supervisor and I prepped Jamie for our ride—by putting the thick leather belt around his waist so we could attach his cuffed hands to the front before cuffing his ankles connected to a short chain—Jamie was still the biggest "baddest" guy on the planet.

By procedure, but more so out of respect, during the ride talking is limited to gentle tones so as not to upset someone like Jamie. Yet halfway through the journey all three of us were so filled with nervous energy that we basically joked about our passion for movies, girls, cars, life, sports, more girls, and so on. I had to stop myself from getting too emotional. Here was Jamie, a young man just under eighteen, who deep down was a good person. Away from "all that" he didn't have to act "all that," and *that* was the tragedy. His parents were good, hardworking folks who truly loved their boy. Jamie *was* popular in school, excelled in sports, and everyone knew he could receive a scholarship to any college he desired. Then from there to infinity: girls, a car, house, great career, marriage, children. An unlimited future; *his* future.

But not that day. By the time the three of us were close to the institution, the reality began to sink in with Jamie. On the final turn, when the cold building surrounded by the towering chain-link fence with coils of razors on the top came into view, my supervisor and I pulled over to the side of the road with the excuse of finding some paperwork. Our true intention was to allow Jamie some time to collect himself. Like all the kids, and I do mean *all,* in Jamie's position, it hit him pretty hard. After a few minutes of sobs and heavy breathing from the backseat while the two of us in the front seat pretended we didn't hear anything, in the softest voice Jamie asked himself, "How did I get here? How did it all come to this?"

I instantly wanted to state something to help console Jamie or something hilarious to break the tension, but he answered his own question: "Guess I screwed up. Man, if I could do it all over again, I'd do things different."

Do things differently.

Now don't take this the wrong way. I am in no way trying to be overly melodramatic here. No way. I have seen and experienced a lot in my life. I'm not the smartest guy on the planet, but I've learned more about psychology from working in places like juvenile hall than I did in any classroom. Part of what I've learned is that while most of these "young adults" screwed up, some more serious than others, there were others who were absolutely pure evil, who relished hurting others with glee—murder, rape, arson, drugs, burglary—you name it, they loved it and lived for nothing else. So if I seem a tad mushy about Jamie, I have a valid reason: In the beginning he wasn't all that bad.

Again, my task is to inform you of the realities of the world in order to encourage you to make responsible decisions.

And *that* is exactly my point. It was through Jamie's choice of *not* working things out with his parents, *knowingly* stealing, no longer applying himself in school, adopting new "friends" with a new attitude, and an endless list that spun out of control that physically, mentally, and spiritually led him through the gates of a hard-core "jail" for teens.

You and you alone decide your future and just how far you will go. You want to be happy? You decide. You wish to be miserable? Well, that's your choice, too. Good self-esteem, low self-esteem; good grades, bad grades; close nurturing friends, defiant destructive friends. Hey, it's your choice.

Passive or Positive

If life gets too hard and you want to feel sorry for yourself, that's your option. But don't expect others to jump on your pity-party wagon. Especially folks like army captain Jacqueline Milam and her two children. Five months pregnant at the time, Milam was working on the other side of the Pentagon the morning one of the terrorists' hijacked planes slammed into the building, killing her husband.

Ron Jr., her baby boy born nearly five months to the day of the disaster, reminds Jacqueline of her spouse, and for that she states, "I'm absolutely loving it." The captain goes on to say, "Don't feel sorry for me. I have had and still have more love than others will have in a lifetime." And while she could rightly claim that losing a spouse and raising two children on her own while enduring the rigors of the military life is way too much to bear, to this day Captain Milam still serves in the army and visits the same building where she lost her husband. "I'm not traumatized by the building. The building did not take my husband."

Everybody has to face and endure some form of hardship, like Doug Blevins who lives with cerebral palsy and yet is a kicking coach for the Miami Dolphins! Yes, Mr. Blevins, who is confined to a wheelchair, works for the prestigious National Football League as one of the premier coaches in his field.

Now how in heaven's name did that come about? "Since I was handicapped, I knew I would never play a down," Doug recalls. "But I was set on this goal. I knew whatever I did I couldn't be pretty good at it, I had to be the best in the country."

Doug, who since the eighth grade has studied thousands of games, attended countless seminars, and scrutinized how kickers approached the football and the exact placement of their hands, began his career at the high school level before making it to the big leagues of the NFL. Throughout Mr. Blevins's quest, while others scoffed and said no, Doug chose to smile back and say, "Why not?"

Hmm, do you see the pattern here?

Your life, your choice.

From now on when push comes to shove, when you feel this enormous pressure, mainly from outside sources, take a moment, just a few seconds, to clear your head and think: *If I do this thing now, how can it affect my future? Is this truly what I want to do?* If the answer is yes, well then hunker down, dig deep, and do it! If the answer is no, well then, *duh,* don't do it.

It may be hard the first few times you start to stand up for your personal beliefs. You may be intimidated; you may want to cave in to temptation and take the easy way out or do what everyone else is doing. That feeling is normal. But never, *never* forget that unless someone has that loaded gun to your head and is telling you how to walk, talk, act, or treat others, you and you alone have the power and the wisdom to choose.

So, in everything you do, make your decision for yourself. Just choose wisely.

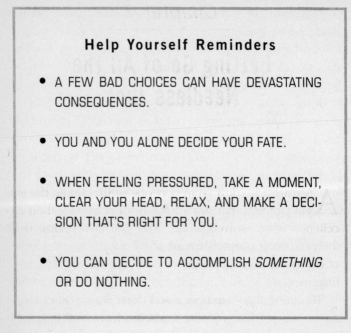

Help Yourself Reminders

- A FEW BAD CHOICES CAN HAVE DEVASTATING CONSEQUENCES.

- YOU AND YOU ALONE DECIDE YOUR FATE.

- WHEN FEELING PRESSURED, TAKE A MOMENT, CLEAR YOUR HEAD, RELAX, AND MAKE A DECISION THAT'S RIGHT FOR YOU.

- YOU CAN DECIDE TO ACCOMPLISH *SOMETHING* OR DO NOTHING.

Chapter 7

Letting Go of All the Needless Junk

As you well know from part one of this book, the single element that stops folks from achieving their excellence is unresolved issues. And you also realize from the preceding chapter that all of us make a great number of decisions, whether good or bad, that we are ultimately responsible for.

To add to that—and because I don't want you to forget this, I suggest that you do yourself a favor and imprint it on your brain—decisions you make now, and I mean *right now,* on how you act, how you think, what you say, how you treat others and yourself, and, most important, how you decide to deal with situations, especially the difficult ones, *will* affect you every single day for the rest of your life!

That's why I admit that at times I do become emotional and very upset when I meet young adults like Jamie. Why? Because, as you've probably already figured out, the Jamies are hurting themselves and literally ruining their lives. Sure there's "collateral damage" to their families, friends, and others, but at the end of the day these Jamies, through *their* choice of not dealing with whatever was gnawing at them in the first place, put *themselves* in their position. And to me that is such a horrible waste.

It's what I call pancaking: one unresolved problem (usually a small one in the beginning) pancaked on top of another on top of another and another, until the person has a towering stack of complications that have become so enormous they're too big to swallow, let alone deal with.

If that weren't enough, don't forget the seemingly everyday things that can get to you, especially on those days when absolutely nothing goes right. Then, on top of that stack of pancaked problems, add all the changes your body is physically and mentally going through. There may be times when you feel as if you can't take anymore.

If you have ever felt this way, it's normal. Trust me on this: It's absolutely normal and completely natural. In fact, if you didn't feel a little frustrated and overwhelmed from time to time, then I'd worry.

That is why it's so critical for you to get into the habit of making the correct choices *now* when dealing with situations as they arise rather than allow them to stack up one by one, eat away at you, get the best of you, and stop you from achieving your greatness.

Learn to Purge

So what can you do to relieve that pressure? Well, rather than avoid, bury, *or* stupidly hope it will somehow magically disappear (which it won't), you need to confront and fully address the situation. And when it comes to the more serious ones, as odd or as gross as this may sound, I want you to "purge" or "vomit" the problems out of your system.

Let me explain this by going back to the Wednesday afternoon that put me on course and changed my life:

> I took the hit from Mother. I didn't mind a bit. I've had worse. I stayed focused. My motivation was the sound of the stove and the bluish purple flames. My reward was watching the black hand from the kitchen clock crawl its way toward the appointed time when my brothers would soon return from their Boy Scout meeting.

> The cycle continued. Mother would hit me, I'd fall to the floor, struggle to stand up, slide my feet as far back as I dared, never quite able to maintain my rigid "position of address" but instead constantly fidget in front of her, stuttering out words that made no sense in my "delusional" state, forcing Mother to repeat the cycle of hitting me between her expletive nouns and never-ending amounts of alcohol over and over and over again.

> And then I heard it. The slight but distinctive sound of the doorknob of the front door turning just before the door itself seemingly burst open. "Mom, I'm home!" It was my brother Ron who was returning home a few minutes early.

> Ron became my savior and with those three words saved my life. I was running out of energy from Mother's attacks and feared she would wise up to my plan at any moment and just pick me up and throw me on the gas stove like a slab of bacon in a sizzling frying pan.

> Yet the one thing Mother had fought for so hard and so long was above all that no one was to ever discover

what went on between us. If someone even dared to ask, the drilled-in instantaneous reply was "I ran into the door" or "I fell down the stairs" or "I'm going through a clumsy stage" or "I got punished for being bad again."

And now the secret, "our secret," was about to be exposed. Looking directly at Mother I could clearly see the blood drain from her face. Her lower lip seemed to quiver. With both hands she clutched her glass of booze as if it would somehow protect her and hide what she did. For a moment she looked ghost white. But before I could think, Mother snatched my pile of clothes in one hand, grabbed me in the other, opened the door that led to the basement/garage, and threw me and my clothes down the stairs.

When I came to my senses, I could see tiny silver stars dancing in front of my eyes. Upstairs, Mother began cooing at Ron in a soft sweet voice. I imagined her giving my oldest brother a loving embrace. All I could do was snap myself back to the cold reality of my situation by dressing myself, while hoping the eerie monsters that I thought lived in the basement didn't devour me.

When the burning sensation from my arm returned, I licked it as the tears streamed down my face. As was my habit after carrying so much shame for so many years, I began to tell myself how apologetic I was that once again I made Mother upset. What a horrible person I was for being so bad all the time. My constant misbehavior forced Mother to drink as much as she did. How sorry I was for every . . .

My throbbing arm interrupted my pity party. With every slight movement from my fingers an electric shock raced up my forearm. And as I had for years, I once again diluted the reality of what had just transpired. "I didn't do it," I muttered to no one. "I didn't do anything. I didn't play on the grass. I didn't get dirty. I didn't talk too loud. I didn't do anything wrong!" I stated in a low, slow, affirming voice.

Now, without replaying my never-ending broken record and without overanalyzing, I sucked in a deep breath a second before everything seemed to seep out from deep inside me: "I get good grades at school. I'm not that stupid. I'm not a bad kid. I try so hard to do everything I can to please *you*. To do my best to do every chore on time. I try so hard to make *you* happy. I'm not the sole reason why Dad and you fight so much, why you're so miserable every moment of every day."

Inspecting the damage to my arm I shook my head to my own self-realization. "I didn't do *this*. It's not all my fault. I didn't do anything. You can't blame me for everything. It's not all me. I don't make you hit me. I'm not putting a gun to your head. I don't make you drink so much. It's not . . ."

A sudden waterfall of tears spilled onto my chest before stinging my arm, but I didn't care. *This* was a long time coming. My world stood still for a few moments. Nothing else mattered. I let everything out. All the years of shame, head games, and countless, deliberately calculated "Santa Claus thinks you're a bad boy" lies I recalled with perfect clarity. I didn't stop. I couldn't stop until I had nothing left within to expel.

After a few minutes, and only after I had nothing left within me to purge, the stream of tears began to ease and my breathing started to settle down. In the darkness of the garage my vision seemed sharper, adjusting to my surroundings. The pulsating burn from my arm remained, but now it seemed more disconnected.

Though physically nothing had changed, something was radically different. My posture became more erect. For some odd reason my self-dignity seemed important. Though my arm still throbbed, my knees wanted to buckle, and my mouth was bone dry, I refused to cave in. I wasn't going to fall down and curl up into a ball and cry myself to sleep. I was tired of sniveling over how much suffering *I* had brought to *Mother*.

It took another minute to discover the transformation. When I realized what had happened, my heart suddenly raced and my vision sharpened more. For the first time *I* had let everything out. I held nothing back. I replayed the countless incidents, seeing the truth for what it *was,* what had truly happened, and I expelled everything I had put off—all that I had diluted and buried for so long.

My mind became a computer of sorts, clicking off how I had stupidly justified to myself because of Mother's brainwashings why I deserved to live in the basement/garage. Why I was expelled from "the family." Why everyone was forbidden to acknowledge my existence, let alone utter my name. Why I was constantly refused food because I didn't do such-and-such chore on time, because I breathed, because I blinked, because some little birdie from school landed on Mother's shoulder to chirp in her ear what I did or didn't do in the school yard. Why every day Mother did whatever she could to outdo herself in her torture and deceit. For years I had swallowed it all, believing that I had brought it *all* on myself and that my condition was solely my fault. But now I saw things differently.

Whatever had been ugly and evil I purged it all out of my system like some horrible sickness. And again, while nothing about me physically changed, the invisible weight that had bore down on me for so long now seemed like a feather.

Staring down at my arm, I knew Mother would not take me to the hospital. I felt certain she probably would not feed me dinner tonight and would most likely attack me for something else before the evening was through. But I didn't feel as terrified or as humiliated as I had a few minutes before. If anything, I felt better, cleaner about myself. And for the moment that was enough to get me through.

Knowing what I know now and looking back at that period in my life, as hard as it was at the time, I'm so glad I finally purged all that junk out of me. I only wish I had made the decision to purge everything sooner. That is why it's so critical for you to understand the importance of choosing to come to terms with situations and getting them totally out of your system.

Get It *All* Out

When you think of purging, I want you to think of it as dealing with a bad stomachache from something you ate. If you keep whatever inside, it's only going to make you more miserable and sick. But when you purge, just like when you get sick and throw up, at the very least you will feel better. You may not be instantly ready for your favorite greasy food or carnival ride, but for now you will be okay.

Keep in mind that I don't mean *purge* literally. I use this word symbolically to help you understand why keeping things inside can harm you emotionally. And I appreciate how hard "emotional purging" can be. Truth be told, it takes a lot out of you. But if you don't regurgitate whatever it is that's ailing you, what choices do you really have?

Recently while on the road someone told me, "Dave, I can't emotionally purge. I have a hard time getting that junk out of my system. What do I do?" I gave it some thought and got an idea. "Okay, here's what you do. If you feel you can't or won't purge that emotional stuff from your system, look at it this way: The next time you go to the bathroom—and I don't mean pee—I want you to "go" in a garbage bag. And every time you have to go, go in that bag. Then wherever life takes you, be it school, work, the movies, the dinner table, and your bed at night, I want you to take that bag with you. All day, every day. And I bet after a few days you'll be more than happy to get rid of all that once and for all!"

As tasteless as that example may sound, think about it: When you see, hear, and are exposed to different things, your brain automatically filters them, whether good or bad. And when you eat, your body does the same with protein, fats, carbohydrates, or anything else to keep you going. Your body naturally absorbs what it needs and gets rid of what it doesn't need, which eventually turns into you know what. And when you get rid of the waste, you get it out of your system, flush it all away, wash your hands, and don't even give a single thought to all that junk. You repeat the cycle over and over until you really don't even give much thought to the intaking, absorbing, filtering, and flushing that goes on.

Get the picture?

And even though emotionally vomiting or purging your problems is not the cure to every situation, at the very least it may be enough to get you through the worst tragedies. A perfect example is 9/11. As the situation unfolded, most of us, including myself, could not believe and even refused to accept the reality and the magnitude as events unfolded. But as the shock wore off, did you become almost mesmerized? Did you and others talk and talk and talk about every aspect of the tragedy to the point of dissecting the events? Did you notice it was the sole topic all day for many, many days, and no matter what you did or who you bumped into, 9/11 was the topic on everybody's minds? For some this process, which is nothing more than healthy purging and is a healthy way of coming to terms, went on for weeks. For some of us it was many, many months until it was finally, completely purged from our system.

The thing I want to impress upon you is that only after buried ill feelings and problems are finally brought to the surface and purged—just as with 9/11 and, on a smaller scale, with my own purging my denial of my mistreatment as a child—can the process of moving forward, healing, and gaining your self-worth and independence truly begin.

And again, while all things do not work for all people, at the very least having the courage to step up to the plate and make the choice to deal with problems that may have been holding you back by getting them out of your system once and for all can only *help* you! If there is something that has been gnawing at you, something you really need to deal with, please find someone you know, someone you trust, and, again, as gross as this may sound, vomit everything out from within your heart. When you do, I guarantee you will feel better. And as time goes by, you will be able to look at things more clearly, which will allow you to make better decisions on how to live your life on your terms.

This is the power of making good decisions. You deal with the bad ones first so that it is easier to deal with the not so bad ones later.

Help Yourself Reminders

- AS CRAZY AS EVERYTHING MAY SEEM, WHEN YOU GET A LITTLE OVERWHELMED, REMEMBER: IT'S NORMAL TO FEEL THIS WAY. JUST TAKE A DEEP BREATH AND DEAL AS BEST YOU CAN WITH LIFE'S CHALLENGES, ONE AT A TIME.

- RATHER THAN PUT OFF OR PANCAKE YOUR PROBLEMS, LEARN TO PURGE EMOTIONALLY WHATEVER IS TRULY BOTHERING YOU.

- DON'T HOLD ANYTHING BACK. MAKE SURE YOU PURGE *EVERYTHING*—ALL THAT JUNK—FROM YOUR SYSTEM, THEN PSYCHOLOGICALLY FLUSH IT AWAY.

Chapter 8

Hate No One

Of all the words you will ever read and of all the things you can ever learn, **hate no one** is the most valuable lesson. Of all the examples in this book, nothing is more important than making the conscious, adamant decision not to become consumed by hatred.

Of all the problems on this planet, animosity—and all that goes with it—is by far the most destructive force known to mankind. Hate consumes and destroys everything in its path. And for what? Revenge? A twisted form of respect? Defensiveness or an endless list of seemingly *reasonable* justifications? And then at the end of one's day, failed dreams, ruined relationships, or the final days of one's life, all that a person can show or be remembered for is a life's worth of devastation and loneliness.

I ask you, is that any way to live? Is that what you truly want or deserve?

The process of hate can begin with something so simple. You're having a bad day, running late, or maybe you forgot to do something important. Then someone makes you mad. That person says one word in a certain tone, with a certain demeanor, at the wrong time that sets you off. You then get mad and stay mad. You do so maybe to prove how deeply hurt you are. You begin to act in a certain way so that you won't be hurt like that again. Maybe you strut rather than walk. You might hang out with those who act like you do. You change things from what you say to what you do and don't do. Then every day whenever you see *that* person or are reminded of *that* thing that sets you off, though you can't remember exactly how it all began, you find it gets easier and easier to stay upset until finally it becomes who you are and what you stand for.

Does any of this sound familiar?

With all that's going on with your body and your developing mind, I cannot begin to tell you how important it is for you not to become consumed by bitterness.

Again, we all say things and do things in the heat of the moment. That's perfectly normal. Everybody does it. Just don't let those frustrations or ill feelings build up and become so powerful that they can cripple you.

The Seduction of Hate

Just look at what hate did to my mother.

After not seeing her since my father passed away seven years prior to midsummer of 1987, I, as a young married man with a ten-month-old son, somehow willed myself to visit Mother face-to-face, hoping to learn some answers to our past.

Even before entering her home, seeing all the charming, nicely maintained houses on the block, I realized Mother's was grossly unkept and overweight, looking

like an abandoned setting from an eerie Hollywood
slasher film. A cold feeling seemed to seep through the
front door. When the door burst open with Mother behind it, an overwhelming stench nearly made me throw
up. Walking up a short flight of stairs behind her, I tried
not to breathe.

If the stench was putrid, the house itself was disgusting. A dried, slimy grease-like dark brown substance
seemed to cling to the walls. I later discovered it was not
worn-out wallpaper but cigarette smoke from years of
Mother's constant reclusive addiction. As I walked up the
staircase, I became concerned that my feet would punch
through the strained wood that had more matted dog
and cat hair than carpet and padding.

After reaching the decayed "living room" and survey-
ing the setting, I couldn't help but think how drastic
Mother's world had changed. Years ago, before things
became too crazy between Mother and me, she was the
epitome of perfection. Her house was seemingly
Camelot, and Mother was, in a word, regal. She took so
much pride in anything that had to do with her home.
Mother was the envy of the block when it came to her
perfectly manicured flowers and to adorning her house
with an endless array of decorations during the holidays.
To say that Mother was meticulous would be an understatement. Specks of dust were not allowed to penetrate
the sanctuary of her proud domain.

But that was years ago, before she gave up on more
than just her residence. When I was a small child,
Mother was a whirlwind of endless activities, at the time
taking my two brothers and me everywhere she could,
which seemed more like an adventure than learning.
Whether we went for a day at the park, to nearby

Chinatown, or camping out with tents in our backyard, Mother dreamt up everything for the love of her family.

Although Mother didn't have fancy clothes, to me she seemed more like my personal Snow White. Her face looked more porcelain than real. Her smile was wide and bright, and her hair held a brilliant shine. As a preschooler, whenever I hugged Mother, I'd try to bury my nose in her hair, thinking it was more like a bouquet of flowers.

And now Mother resembled a walking train wreck. Her soiled attire looked as if she had worn the same outfit for decades. Mother's once smooth face was now hardened and dark red, with blotchy weltlike marks. Mother's flaky hair seemed glued to the sides of her face in clumps. Yet the thing that literally took my breath away was the dank, sweaty odor that emanated from her shabby chair. At first I thought the smell belonged to one of her unkept animals, but then I realized the odor was from my own mother.

Her eyes seemed cloudy and withdrawn. Mother's grayish reddened swollen hands constantly trembled, revealing just how far Mother had plummeted. Studying me studying her, Mother wooed in a low voice. "Arthritis. You can't imagine the pain I'm in. No one can."

I sat down in a chair next to her. Part of me could not accept that I was not only one-on-one with but inches away from the person who seemingly a lifetime ago, with sickening glee, tried to kill me while humiliating me to no end. It was pathetic how Mother had allowed herself to deteriorate. As curious as I was to find answers to my past, I had no idea where to begin. Then out of some sense of etiquette and sympathy for Mother's condition, I wasn't quite certain *if* I should even pry. Scanning Mother from head to toe, I became numb to what transpired between us. I became consumed with nothing but absolute pity for her. I couldn't bring myself to the reality that this person in front of me was my biological mother.

As soon as my youngest brother darted from the house to play outside, leaving Mother and me alone, the mood between us suddenly changed. In a low but confidently stern voice Mother stated that one time when she had stabbed me and then refused to take me to the hospital for fear of exposure, the incident was nothing more than a minor accident. (When it happened, I knew Mother never meant to hurt me as much as she meant to scare me, as she had countless times in the past, by waving a knife in front of me.) A little mistake. A tiny misunderstanding. No big deal. Yet it was her nonchalant tone, the look on her face, and Mother's body language that woke me from my trance. Mother was not asking for my forgiveness as much as she was informing me to dismiss the bloody episode entirely. It took only another few seconds for me to realize that if I did, then I would be ignoring—and, more so, should be ignoring—the endless series of incidents between us. Mother then flashed me a look of displeasure because I had not instantly fallen to my knees to humble myself before her.

Now numb to her words as well as the nauseating setting, Mother spilled out a seemingly rehearsed justification that "The Boy," "It," was simply bad. "The Boy's" voice was too loud. "The Boy" was always trying to steal something to eat. "The Boy" was the source for everything wrong in her life, and therefore "The Boy" simply deserved whatever discipline Mother felt necessary.

I couldn't believe my ears. I was smart, smarter than

her. I was trustworthy, and overall I was a good person, I thought to myself. But once again I allowed myself to be taken in, to be manipulated by Mother. After years of torture, humiliation, and endless head games, I had had enough of her shit. Her dramatic show of self-pity and justification of how she *had* to treat me as she did was the last straw.

As Mother rambled nonstop about "The Boy" this and "The Boy" that, I began to imagine what it would be like if I gave her a little of what she gave me. What if, I fanta-sized, I tricked Mother by kidnapping her and then lock-ing her away in some seedy motel with no light, food, heat, or any contact with the outside world? What if I de-prived "Her" of everything but herself? Then I'd make "Her" feel all the pain, the loneliness, and the humilia-tion that she had relished against me all those years. Having fed off the pain of others, she would literally be driven insane by "Her" isolation.

The more I sat back in my worn chair, the better I felt. My mind spun with elaborate plots of give-and-take that could drag on as long as I savored. I began to feel I could do this. *I'd show "Her,"* I told myself. *If "She" died, "She" died. What would I care? Screw "Her." And if I got caught, well . . . I could say*—I justified to myself—*it was some sort of post-traumatic stress, a form of insanity brought on after years of horrendous abuse. Then, at my day in court, I'd play the sympathy card while whimper-ing, 'Your Honor, I was mistreated. She had it coming. I didn't know any better. Society let me down. It's their fault. Besides, what have I done that hundreds of thou-sands of others in my situation haven't already commit-ted?'*"

As the coldness left my body, it became replaced

with a sense of warmth. A feeling of control. A sensation of power. But during my little revenge fantasy I pictured my son, not even two years old, in the courtroom. My boy standing in the aisle watching the fate of his father in shackles, a broken figure of a man who had stood for stopping the cycle of hate, for living all those years to better himself, providing for his family while ensuring his son had more opportunity than he had had, and helping others who, too, had suffered. But he *had to* have his revenge, not only throwing his life away but ruining the lives of others in the process.

What kind of legacy would that leave to my son? What kind of values would that teach him? What impact would my selfless, cowardly decision have on my own flesh and blood?

Clearing my head I came back to the reality of Mother's continuing rambling. I looked at her, realizing that if I ever harmed her, if I had my revenge, I would in fact not only continue the cycle of hate and violence but most likely elevate it to a new level. I would become exactly like her. And that was something I could not do. Years ago when Mother burned my arm on the gas stove, I made a promise in the bottom of a cold, dark basement. With blisters forming on my arm I raised it toward my chest and vowed to God and myself that I would be the best person I could. I would never quit on myself, and I would do whatever I could not to become like "Her."

I'll stop here for a moment to tell you what I'm sure you already know. Either way, I want you to highlight this or write it down for future reference: **For someone to**

hurt you, someone must have hurt that person as well. When you repeat the cycle of hate and destruction—whether it is toward yourself or others—*you are* choosing to continue the cycle. **You** are. Again, unless someone has a firearm to your head, it is basically your choice and yours alone. And if you choose to "pay back" or show others how tough you are for most of your everyday life, when does your journey end? How much is enough? Then in the end what will all that accomplish? Do you really think that being the biggest, baddest person on the planet will gain the respect and loyalty of others through fear and intimidation?

I don't mean to step on toes here, but let me ask if you know anyone who is the biggest, baddest person on your block or even in your city? In what town or part of the country does that person live? In all the other regions of the nation or parts of the world, that bad person would be swallowed up in the blink of an eye. The point is: Joe Blow might be the biggest, baddest person in, let's say, Wahoo, Nebraska, but that's Wahoo, Nebraska, not Los Angeles, or Harlem, New York, or other places across America that are considered war zones. Trust me, there's always someone "badder" than you.

Are You Bad Enough?

But let's say you know someone who is actually that tough, that bad, who is gonna show the world how big he is and make others pay for his misery. Let's take a look at history to see how others who were *really* hard cases did for themselves. There once was a fellow named Hitler who hated and destroyed anyone who wasn't a part of *his* delusional "master race." He had a friend, Mussolini, and between them their legacy became one of invading country after country while bringing death and destruction to millions. Do you know anybody *that* bad?

Where are they now? Mussolini was captured and hung upside down from a public lamppost. Hitler, well, he was such a tough guy that as the Allied Forces closed in on his country's capital of Berlin, Hitler had young boys not even in their preteen years fight them off, and being the coward that he was, he hid out in an underground bunker before committing suicide. And don't get me started on that megalomaniac Stalin, the premier of the Soviet Union who through his hatred and paranoia killed and imprisoned more than 12 million of his own countrymen, women, and children.

To take liberty and paraphrase an old saying, *Those who do not know their history **are** doomed to repeat it*. How do you or others you know fit into that statement?

To stop the cycle of that kind of hatred and devastation, after World War II the United Nations was formed. And while at times this body of nations acts more like squabbling siblings and may seem as if they can't break up a cookie fight at a Girl Scout meeting, they are in fact determined to prevent another uprising of someone like Hitler.

But let's say you're not too knowledgeable when it comes to history (which tells me you need to study more) or you may wish to believe that past events don't affect you. I'm sure you're familiar with current events when it comes to Osama Bin Laden and Saddam Hussein. When American forces finally caught the great and powerful dictator, uh, I mean President Hussein, he was hiding like the coward he was in a spider hole. Though armed to the teeth with over half a million dollars and a handgun, he didn't fire a shot and gave up after nervously shouting, "Don't shoot! Don't shoot!" I heard he was so scared that he peed on himself. As for Bin Laden, if he's not dead, he's probably living the high life in some darkened cave or underground sewer. I guess you gotta be tough to kill innocent folks and live like a rat. Wow! I'm impressed. Aren't you?

But let's say you don't have those lofty goals of world domination or international terrorism. Right now you lack the capital to finance an army. But don't fret. As I've stated before, this is America where with hard work, sacrifice, and a little luck anything is possible. So if you or someone you know chooses to hate and do all that goes with it on a more advanced level, I'm sure that person will get away with it for a while. But in this arena one thing leads to another, and sooner or later (if that person doesn't end up dead) that person will definitely end up living the rest of his or her days in a cell or some kind of prison.

You might say, "Come on, Dave. Aren't you being extreme?" Good question. My answer? *No!* I've been to adult and juvenile institutions all over the nation for years, and I've seen it all. Most of the time when folks have the guts to open up to what's really the issue, it's usually the same pattern, not a single element but a pattern:

Some unresolved issue leads to . . .

An intense hatred that leads to . . .

A sense of revenge.

For the most part, once a breakthrough was made, these folks came to realize for themselves not only how destructive their lives were but also how tremendous that burden of hatred was for them to carry.

For some it's a form of protection, a sense of control. I can understand that you don't want folks to take advantage of you, but in the long run it will ruin you. And while you may not be the next Hitler or Saddam Hussein, your hatred, your thirst for revenge will destroy your life. And that's something I and others who truly know you don't want for your life.

On the scale of hatred look carefully how it ate away at my own mother. As disgusting as it was for me that day to sit with her, once again she taught me a great deal.

> Mother just wouldn't shut up. She went on and on and on about how the world had been against her all these years.
>
> "Oh, you think you had it bad. Let me tell you something. My mother, my own mother abused me. She'd beat me. Lock me in a closet for hours at a time. And once she didn't feed me for days. You can't even begin to imagine!"

Do you understand how my mother's hatred was not only passed on to me but amplified in the process? My mother was beaten by her mother, so she conjured up games to torture me. Mom missed a few meals, and in one period she refused me food for two weeks. Mother was kept in a closet, and when I was not in school or performing chores, I lived and slept in the basement. That's how the "disease" of hate spreads. It's always more. And it never ends. It's never enough revenge.

Am I getting through to you?

I nodded that I indeed understood Mother. Yes, I could imagine what it felt like.

Even as a young man there was a lot I knew about my perpetrator. When I "interviewed" my mother's mother, Grandma relayed in the same venomous tone as my mother did (something Mother unknowingly copied from my grandmother) how Mother was seemingly always unappreciative, that she had to have things her way, that my mother as a young person would never listen to my grandmother when it came to living her life as Grandma insisted. And while my grandmother, whom I admired in many ways and who raised two children alone in the middle of a horrible depression in the once extremely conservative Salt Lake City area, loudly proclaimed to me that she never abused my mother, something told me different.

"You just can't understand. No one can," Mother half whimpered, playing it to the hilt while her swollen fingers, which resembled sausages on both hands, trembled as she tried to clutch what I called her medicine: a tall glass of pure cheap vodka.

After fighting to bring her "medicine" to her lips and then trying to balance the glass as she placed it back down, Mother explained in a low whisper that she began drinking as a young teen, sneaking out to have a few sips with some girlfriends from school. She drank to feel better, and she drank craving acceptance from others. "I felt pretty," Mother stated, looking down at her swollen feet. "I was happy. Everybody liked me. It helped numb the pain. You understand?"

Indeed I did. All I could do was nod. In the years I've dealt with Mother, in the rarest of moments she would slip from her facade and speak without fear of judgment, as if I were her confessor. It was this insight into Mother that I had prayed for when she spoke like this when I was a child. But it was always fleeting; her wall of defense slammed shut before Mother could realize her breakthrough. "By the time I was fifteen, I couldn't survive without it. My medicine," Mother slowly confessed.

Part of me saw this broken little girl trapped inside a bloated vengeful woman. Part of me wanted to drop to my knees and hug Mother's pain, loneliness, and all the junk-filled baggage she had carried for all those years away. Back then women were still treated like second-class citizens. Alcoholism was not discussed, and above all, when it came to abuse, what happened in someone's house stayed in that person's house. The cardinal rule was never, ever expose a family's dirty little secret.

As I now studied my mother's every move, analyzing to see if she was once again acting out a dramatic game or was she truly trying to come to terms with her past, I realized back then, in her day, there was no one to go to, no avenues of consolation. Back then, as time marched forward through Mother's unresolved past, her feelings of intense hatred mixed in with her addiction, and she used all of it as a shield. I felt her outcome was probably determined years before I was even conceived. With all those elements, to me my mother was a human time bomb.

Snapping out of her self-induced trance, Mother leaned back in her chair with her eyes ablaze. "But I showed her. She's never going to tell me what to do. She's not going to run my life. I hate that damn bitch of a mother. I hate 'Her,' my father, Dan [her brother], his entire family, that excuse of a husband, 'That Boy,' his nosy teachers, that principal, that neighbor Charlene. I hate them. I hate them all.

"But I showed her," Mother emphasized with a raised finger as she nearly coughed up a lung. "I showed them all. No damn person is going tell *me* what to do. No one's going to control me."

"Yeah," I told myself, watching Mother's bloated crimson face and twitching fingers as she sat on her infested throne in her self-made pathetic house of horrors. "No one or nothing is ever going to *control* you!" I thought to myself. "Yeah, right." Here's a person who practically pees on herself and has the shakes 24/7 until she gets her fix and whose only form of control as her life goes by is what channel she selects on her outdated TV. Look how far your hate took you. Quite the life!

I must stop now and confess something to you. I've been involved in many threatening situations, and I've personally been exposed to mankind's dark side, but to this day, after all the troubled young adults and hard-core adult prisoners I've met, and even some of the trashy residences I've stepped into, my own mother and her home are by far the most disturbing and the most disgusting of them all.

Please understand, none of this gives me pleasure. I'm not trying to run my mother down. Nor am I holding a pity party for myself or my courageous brothers who endured my mother's madness as well. I *am,* however, making an effort to go into elaborate details about a real person's life, to convey to you just how your decision of hate can destroy your life.

Do you now realize that at your age, as much as hate

(in its early stages) *seems* to be a form of defense or a way of protecting you, it in fact creates the opposite effect?

I beg you, please, learn from my mother's vengeful, wasted life.

Hate Is a Cancer

Because of Mother's decision concerning how she'd live her life, I have strongly come to the conclusion that hate, if not dealt with, is a form of cancer that spreads and kills all day, every day, one day at a time. And like any deadly disease, it spreads and destroys those who come in contact with the "virus" of hatred. Over time your hatred will dominate your life, but you will become a carbon copy of what you once hated, **if not more.**

Now that you know the type of person who nearly killed me and made life hell for others around her, and you have had a peek into all that my mother endured, ask yourself: What did all that hate do *for* her? Did all her time and energy spent on hatred help her? Did my mother's choice of revenge make her life better? Was she really in *control* of her life? Or did my mother's unresolved issues, coupled with the escapism of her booze, added with her intense hatred, take charge of her life? And the final question: Was my mother a happy, successful, fulfilled person?

Am I making myself clear to you?

So what do you do? Part of the solution (as related in the first part of this book) is having the resolve to deal with your issues as soon as you can. You address them, you make logical decisions, and you completely purge whatever troubles you—whether it's by sitting down and talking it out, writing a letter you never mail, or yelling at that vacant chair—and then you move on, you let go. You will not go far in your future if you are stuck in the past.

The Power to Forgive

When it comes to working through the more disturbing emotional situations, such as resentment or revenge, the most powerful remedy is *the power of forgiveness*. When you forgive, **you're** taking a stand; **you are** making the choice that you *will not* be consumed by negative experiences. You are putting yourself in control by making the decision not to repeat the cycle of hatred and destruction. You are acting in a manner of great courage rather than following the trait of revenge or despair, which is a sign of weakness. That above all you have the guts to right a wrong.

By forgiving you are breaking the chains that can keep you enslaved with your unfortunate past forever. Think about that again. By your decision to forgive you are freeing yourself from former experiences that can dominate you, as they did my mother, for the rest of your days. Simply put, you deserve to be happy, you deserve to live life on your terms, but you can only do so when you truly let go of all that negative baggage. All of it!

And as much as it takes guts, forgiveness also takes time. Just like grieving over the loss of a loved one or a relationship that didn't work out, in time it becomes easier while making your life better. Just like getting dressed, brushing your teeth, going to school or work, you make forgiveness a part of your everyday lifestyle.

Another important if not vital part about your choice to forgive is that it makes you more mature. Much more. You will soon see things differently from those stuck in their own mire. By that, you'll observe others who, by their own choice, hold grudges and act out, not even realizing why they do what they do; but what matters for them is they carry that resentment with them. In your case, when faced with a tough situation, you'll treat others not with vengeance or hatred but with the strength of compassion. And through the passage of time, those same folks who have built walls around themselves will seem as if they've stood still, if not traveled backward, in areas of their lives while you have surged well beyond.

Always Remember

By asking you to forgive I am in no way saying you have to forget. Through your maturity of forgiveness you will learn that whatever happened to you or against you is in fact a very, very small fraction of your entire life. Even to this day with all the blessings I've been given— freedom from my mother, the love and encouragement while in foster care, the wondrous adventures flying for the air force, my career that often seems like some Hollywood fable, and, most important, the love and devotion of a beautiful wife and even the act of playing a simple game of catch with my son—I *never* forget where I came from.

Never forget the bad times or those challenging situations when you stood tall against the odds with a sense of righteousness, so you can appreciate the good times. Once as a child when I was still living in the basement of my mother's house and hadn't eaten for days, I stole some frozen piecrust from the nearby freezer. The morsel was only the size of a dime, but after warming it up in the palm of my hands before swallowing it, I felt as if I was the king of this gigantic feast. Why? Because it was more than I had yesterday. Even as I write these precious words to you in my hope of waking you up, to have you better yourself, realize I can now gorge myself with any fancy meal of my choosing, but still that tidbit of piecrust was the best meal I've ever eaten.

Years ago while appearing on a premier national talk show, the host gently probed if I could ever forgive my mother. Without hesitation I replied, "How could I not?" The host gasped, not understanding, until I stated, "With all that my mother went through, the decisions she made within the context of society for its time, she never had much of a chance."

So for me when does it end? How much is enough? It ends by realizing how destructive a force hate can be. It's enough seeing my mother existing in her own filth, carrying the torch of despair with her to her grave. Through years of humiliations and despair I've *learned* a great deal.

The afternoon I found out my mother passed away, I was on flight line duty with the air force. Dressed in my flight gear in front of a stunned messenger, I knelt down on one knee and said, "Thank God. Let 'Her' finally rest in peace." For years, even as a child, I had forgiven my perpetrator. I had always known that as much as she was evil, my "mommy" was simply sick. But the moment I uttered her eulogy, an enormous weight was lifted from my soul. At that moment I felt cleansed. I didn't need to punish myself and others through a lifelong quest or beat myself up trying to decipher the question "Why me?" I didn't need to become the next serial killer or drug-addicted scumbag to have my revenge or be controlled by a narcissistic need for escapism. I just needed to choose to forgive the person who hurt me as much as she was harmed.

This is the time in your life in which the decisions you make now and how you address situations will either strengthen you or haunt you for the rest of your life. I implore you to be mature enough to be of good mind and good heart, to be better than me, and to learn from the life and times of my mother. With all my heart I pray you are strong enough to **choose to forgive.**

Help Yourself Reminders

- OVER TIME THE SEDUCTION OF HATE LEADS TO DESPISING ANY AND ALL THINGS, WHICH INCLUDES THOSE YOU ARE CLOSEST TO, EVEN YOURSELF.

- EVEN THE "BADDEST OF THE BAD" END UP WITH ONLY THEIR WASTED, VIOLENT, DESTRUCTIVE LIVES.

- HATE *IS* A CANCER THAT EVENTUALLY KILLS EVERYTHING IT COMES IN CONTACT WITH.

- WHEN YOU FORGIVE, IT DOESN'T MEAN YOU FORGET. IT NOT ONLY BREAKS THOSE CHAINS THAT HAVE KEPT YOU A PRISONER OF YOUR PAST BUT GIVES YOU A MATURE PERSPECTIVE, ALLOWING YOU TO MOVE FORWARD—BUT NOW WITH A SENSE OF POSITIVE CONTROL.

- NEVER FORGET THE BAD TIMES SO YOU CAN SAVOR THE GOOD ONES.

Part Three

PERSONAL RESOLVE

Chapter 9

Keeping Your Faith

What upsets me the most are those folks who seemingly throw up their hands in a gesture of complete surrender at the smallest of life's challenges. These same individuals *justify* their lifestyles with pitiful excuses: "Everyone's against me." "It's my family's fault." "I had a horrible childhood." "I fell in with the wrong crowd." "My parents split up." "Life's not fair." "It's their fault." "So-and-so has it all." "I got a bad back." Blah, blah, blah—whatever.

I see this a lot with folks in their late thirties and forties who believe life has unfairly passed *them* by; they refuse to better themselves because they believe life will never get any better. Therefore, the only thing they can do is rationalize their situation in a series of nothing more than excuses. (Remember my mother, a broken woman, sitting in her repulsive home and how she tossed out an endless list of justifications while stewing in her own hatred?)

I also see this same attitude beginning to develop in young adults your age. The reason it makes me so upset, if not extremely pissed off, is that unlike those who have wasted most of their lives, **you** have **so much** ahead of you. Don't forget: If you quit on yourself now, you will live with your regret, your shame, and your inability to better yourself. You will be tossing away all your dreams every single day for the next seventy thousand days. And that's all day every day.

You think life's too hard to battle back from adversity? Hold on a sec and think of Lance Armstrong who went on to win six—not one or two but six—back-to-back Tour de France races. And that's after surviving testicular cancer just so he could train to compete in a bone-crushing two-thousand-mile race through the high-peaked mountains of France. For a man who believes every second counts, he applies those words to his beautiful children more than to his races. Mr. Armstrong also quips, "Pain is temporary. Quitting lasts forever."

On a side note I'll tell you something many adults will never confess: Most of us are not, I repeat, *are not* trying to breed the "perfect child." For the most part we really don't care if you get all A's in class, if you hit that home run in the bottom of the ninth inning with two outs, if you score that goal in the soccer game, or if you get first place in track. *However,* if you are *capable* of A's and turn in D's or if you take a half swing when up at bat rather than a full swing, those who raised you should not be pleased with your actions, nor should you. You are developing the habit of cheating yourself!

When you commit to something, I expect you to give it your all. I don't care if it's keeping your word about being home at a certain time, cleaning your room, helping with the household chores, being a good friend, playing sports, studying for a test, or anything in your life that has the least bit of importance. **Once you commit, I don't want you to quit!** When you pledge to do something, I want you to develop that mental habit—just as you would when it comes to crunch time in sports, that big exam, or something that's important to you—to give it everything. That means every fiber of your being, every ounce of strength. Whatever brain cells you have, I want you to give it your absolute all. Period. Just like getting dressed, driving a car, or even walking when you were a little tyke, develop the routine now, and you will soon see how far it will strengthen and advance you in the course of your life.

So, when you're running in the game of life and when—not if but **when**—you slip and fall, I expect you to get up, brush yourself off, and complete your task. Even when you're physically or psychologically bruised and you have to drag yourself across the finish line, knowing full well you're in last place, give it **everything** you have.

There can be more victory in trying, no matter the outcome, knowing you gave it your all than never making the attempt to achieve.

As a young adult you are at the crossroads of your life. When it comes to life's little bumps in the road, you have only two options: 1) Bury your face in the sand, throw out excuses, "defend" yourself through ill feelings, and live the sad life like my mother and countless other pathetic souls like her, or 2) Learn something from the situation and take positive control by pushing aside those challenges that can only pull you down . . . then press on.

Commit to Prevail

Remember: Everybody—and I do mean *everybody*—falls down. It's only picking yourself up that truly matters.

If anybody knows the meaning of those words it's the internationally acclaimed and most decorated skater of her generation, the lovely Michelle Kwan. In the 2002 Winter Olympics she just missed another gold medal, *but* because she nearly fell from one of her triple flips, Michelle received the bronze medal instead. In the previous Olympic Games she fell in one of her routines, but rather than crying in front of 65 million viewers from all over the world, Michelle pushed aside all that anxiety, all that pressure; she applied herself and focused more than ever to take home the gold. Asked if she would put herself through a grueling third Olympic Games and all the constant training it entails, Ms. Kwan replied, "I can't guarantee anything. But skating is such a wonderful sport. Who knows?" Personally, I think we'll all see Michelle not only at the Games but at the winners' podium again. I think for those like Ms. Kwan, it's never about the "gold" as much as it is about never giving in when one slips and falls.

Even at the seemingly worst of times, when it appears that things can never get better, I swear to you that whatever challenges you're facing now, they are only a tiny minuscule portion of your entire life, and when you deal with those challenges, **they** only make you **stronger.** To quote a dear friend who never caved in when the going got tough, Richard Paul Evans, the author of the legendary, number one international bestselling book *The Christmas Box:* "It is in the darkest of skies in which the brightest stars can be seen."

As I write these words of sincere encouragement to you, I honestly confess that I never, ever dreamt that I'd ever be able to experience all the incredible things that I've been blessed with in the course of my life, especially when I consider the depths of where I came from and all that *could* have stood in my way. Again, I never saw myself as a victim. (Don't forget: Attitude is everything.) And, again, I simply did what I had to do. For the most part I didn't quit on myself. Without pomp and circumstance, I credit much of my success to the help of others, luck, and the grace of God.

And my triumph also came from that afternoon when I was burned on the gas stove. Again, it was *that* single event that became my mental fork in the road. It was that ordeal that enabled me to find my resolve which changed how I would address and deal with obstacles for the rest of my life.

Every day Mother did whatever she could to outdo herself in her torture and deceit. For years I had swallowed it all, believing that I had brought it *all* on myself and that my condition was solely my fault. But now I saw things differently.

What had been ugly and evil, I vomited all out of my system like some horrible sickness. And, again, while nothing about me physically changed, the invisible weight that had worn me down for so long now seemed like a feather.

Staring down at my arm, I knew Mother would not take me to the hospital. I felt certain she probably would attack me for something else before the evening was through, but I didn't feel as terrified, as humiliated as I had a few minutes before. If anything, I felt better, cleaner about myself. And for the moment that was enough to get me through.

Yet in that moment of clarity as my breathing slowed,

I examined my arm. From the palm of my hand to beyond my elbow, blisters began to form. As cold as I became standing at the base of the garage staircase, part of me was fascinated by the heat from my sores. Out of curiosity I twitched my fingers. Suddenly an electric-like jolt shot through the length of my arm, forcing tears to burst from my eyes. Clamping my mouth shut, all I could do was gently cradle my injured arm with my free one while telling myself everything would be fine.

Through the darkness my eyes adjusted. I could see the small, coiled, blackened hairs on my arm and carefully blew them off. The sensation felt good. Taking another moment to think about my actions, I licked my arm, hoping my saliva would help cool the growing blisters. Applying too much pressure to one, I again flinched, cried, cradled, and blew cold air on the wound, repeating the process all over again.

Taking a moment, I studied my arm to see exactly how bad it was becoming. As much as I tried, I could not block out the throbbing pain. I wanted to cry and scream all at the same time until I passed out. But then suddenly it hit me: If I could feel my arm, *I was alive,* which meant I was not dead. I did it; I won! With all at her disposal, with all her planning and doing her best to hurt me as much as she liked, Mother hadn't succeeded. *I* had bought a few seconds of precious time, *I* took control of the situation, *I* thought ahead, *I* focused. *I* won.

The excitement of my revelation helped ease the pain from my arm. For the first time in my life I felt truly proud of myself. *I* did it. In the midst of all that was happening to me, I came up with a plan. I didn't back down. I took a few hits, but in the end I was still standing. I'm here. I'm alive. And if I could outthink Mother on what had just happened, if I could take what she dished out, if I could live through all that I had for all those years as a little kid . . . Oh, my God! What could I *not* possibly do?"

Take a second and think about my personal example. Now, I want you to remember all the situations *you've* been through. As a young adult, with all that you've experienced thus far, how did *you* do it? How did you get through it all? Think about this. With little or no help, without any specialized training, without a college degree or guidance from someone like coach Phil Jackson from the L.A. Lakers giving you the play-by-play rundown, if you can survive all that you have already, tell me, what in heaven's name can you not achieve?

The answer? **Nothing.** Not a darn thing. There is nothing you cannot achieve.

Overcoming the Hard Stuff

Think about this. If you can survive cancer, don't you think you can deal with the flu? If you can endure a painful divorce, a troubled childhood, or whatever problems you may be facing at school and all the trivial situations and social pressures of a young adult, again with little or no help, don't you think as you grow older—while maturing in ways that others who don't commit to being responsible won't—that you will in fact be all the stronger, all the wiser because of your former experiences? Hmm?

The answer is: **Hell, yes!**

Live this, learn this, love this: All that you may be going

through now or have already experienced—as horrible, as filthy, as dark, and as excruciatingly hard as it may seem or has been—is only a small, I repeat, a very small, tiny, tiny fragment of your *entire* life! If you feel down or ashamed, don't! Don't cave. Don't give in to fear or anxiety. Don't judge yourself or your situation on how others may have reacted or think of you. **Don't. Don't get depressed, feel embarrassed, be too hard on yourself, or even give a hoot about how others may or may not think about you. Don't. And above all, no matter the odds or however long it takes, don't you quit on yourself!** If anything, *wake up* to the fact that you've already overcome so much and gone so far, simply by applying good common sense while not buckling. And remember that during the course of your life those situations **will** only make you stronger.

That's the truth!

Take a good look into your past and ask yourself how in heaven's name did *you* do it? How in the world did you survive day by day, moment by moment, and *still* go to school, work, maintain friendships, live at home, and do all those normal everyday things of life?

The answer: **You just did. You simply did whatever you had to do.**

Well then, if you can accomplish all that without any help or training, then I expect you to keep your chin up, strengthen your resolve, maintain your focus, and forge ahead. And when things get a little tough, as they will, tell yourself, "I've been through worse. I survived more junk than this, and I'm still here! I can do this!"

Get guttural. Get mean. Dig deep.

Bottom line: **Commit to prevail.**

It's More About You Than Anything Else

Here's another way of looking at it. Let's say at the beginning of your school semester you sign up for track. Your coach enters the room and booms, "Thanks for coming. But just because you showed up doesn't mean you get to join the team. First, I gotta see what you're made of. If you pass all the tests, you get a slot. It's that simple. In the end I'll teach you more about yourself than simply running.

"Now, just so you know I'm not full of hot air"—he suddenly opens his jacket to reveal several gold medals—"I'm pretty good at what I do.

"So now that I have your attention, here's what we're gonna do. I hope you came prepared, 'cause today we're gonna take a little stroll. Today each of you is going to run ten miles."

Suddenly your heart is in your throat as you discover *this* is far more than you bargained for. The coach can't be serious. Ten miles? How am I . . . ?

Others around you voice their opinions, but only in opposition. Some whine with outrage. "No way. Man, this sucks. I ain't gonna do it. Ten miles? Ain't no one gonna make me. . . ."

"Quiet!" the coach barks. "You want to join the team, you want to earn your letter for your jacket, well, these are the rules, my rules, and this is only the beginning. If you think this is too much for you, there's the door. No one's forcing you to stay.

"Now I can pretty much tell by most of your reactions who has it and who doesn't. Some of you have already given up without taking a single step. If you think ten miles is rough, how are you gonna complete your task when it's freezing cold or raining or when your muscles are as tight as a drum and your feet feel like blocks of cement? What are you gonna do when you're out there on your own in the middle of nowhere and you've got no choice? Ain't no one gonna pick you up and carry you.

"I'm here to teach endurance. I teach strength. Resolve. Not here"—he points at the bicep muscles in his arm—"but here," and the coach points at his heart. "Now that's what it's all about. So if you think you have what it takes, let's go. And just so you don't think I'm a hard case, I'll be with you every step of the way. Understand, I don't have to do it. I've earned my place, I know what I'm made of a thousand times over. But you're that important to me. So let's go!"

Wow, that's only Monday. On Tuesday, Wednesday, Thursday, and Friday it's more of the same—a grueling ten miles each and every day. That's about 26,400 strides for each foot for each day!

The following Monday you notice how placid the class has become. It seems more somber, more centered, less prankish, less bravado. More mature. The coach enters calmly, motioning for everyone to gather around him as he kneels. In a low but still serious voice he states, "Look around. The class is not even half the size it was last week. Why is that? Could it be that some just didn't have it? For whatever reason or excuse, they didn't really give it their all?" He gestures again at his heart. "Come on, tell me. How hard is it to simply put one foot in front of the other, then another and another and another? Can't be all that difficult. You've all been doing it since you were rug rats.

"In case you haven't already guessed, it's your attitude I'm speaking of, ladies and gentleman." He further explains: "If you tell yourself you can't do something or how hard or impossible your task is, your body will automatically obey your mind's command. It's called 'follow through.' If you step out on the field telling yourself you're gonna get creamed, well, don't be surprised when you do.

"The same thing applies when it comes to taking a test. Have you ever gotten all tensed up before an exam, telling yourself how hard it's going to be even though you've studied for it? Then the big day comes and you lose your footing, which leads you to blowing the exam.

"But"—he raises a finger as he switches gears—"did you notice last week when you were out there running that you thought about giving up? Come on, I know you did. It's completely natural. Your body and your mind just aren't used to that sort of punishing endurance. But look around. Somehow all of you here dug deep, finding something you didn't know you had. Guts. Maturity. Tenacity. Whatever the word, you've got it. Now that's what I'm talking about!" He emphasizes this with a thunderous clap of his hands. "You brushed aside your doubts and your pain, and used your fear, your anxiety, your issues to push you and propel you ahead. I call that the slingshot effect. When it comes to running and life in general, it's you and the road. You're out there all alone. You take whatever thoughts, doubts, or fears with you when you're on that long winding road.

"One foot in front of the other. Persistence. That's the ticket.

"So whenever you hear that little voice attempting to

sabotage what you've already worked so hard for, trying to tell you how much things suck, how unfair things are, how much it hurts, *turn it off!* The more you listen to that voice, the more it will **dominate you.** The more it will take over. The more it will **win over you.** The more it will sap your strength, your dreams, your ambitions, and your greatness. Are you getting this?" he asked.

"So here's what you do. When you're out there all alone doing your thing and start to feel you have nothing left, when the pain begins to build or that doubting voice begins to take over, tell yourself—hell, yell at yourself—this one thing: 'One more step. Just one more step.' Then tell yourself another step. Then another and another and another. Pretty soon you'll become so focused on your task that it will push aside any pain and doubts you had in the first place.

"As I told you all in the beginning, *this* is more than about running track. This is more about strengthening your mind and developing good solid habits than anything else. Try that technique the next time you're doing homework, your exercises at the gym, or anything else that requires solid effort on your part.

"All right," the coach now says with another slap of his hands, "let's get down to business. As you are all aware, last week was a little challenging. Get ready because this week each and every one of you . . ." Now after all his charming advice your throat again tightens and your anxiety level goes up a few notches as you begin to imagine yourself running, straining, coughing your way through fifteen or maybe twenty miles. Coach Hardnose finishes: "Every one of you is going to run—are you ready for this?—twenty miles!"

You close your eyes as your brain screams, *No way! There is no way I can run twenty miles a day! I can't do it!*

"What's the problem?" the coach grumbles. "Last week you all ran fifty miles. This week you have to run only twenty miles. For goodness' sake," he says with a grin, "that's four miles a day. Come on, are you telling me that after running ten miles a day you can't run a measly four miles?" You realize your apprehension was all for naught. "Well, then," he teases, "what do you say? Can you do it?"

Suddenly you and everyone else around realizes you can do it and do so with relative ease.

And why? Because you've already accomplished so much more.

My premise in that example is that there is no reason for someone who has already been through so much to even think about quitting on themselves, especially when something smaller and less trivial pops up.

In the final analysis, at the end of the day when you're alone, you have to tell yourself and educate yourself: "Hey, I've been through worse than this." And do so knowing you did what you had to do to endure with *limited* resources. Then understand as you grow older that you *will be* all the wiser and far more mature. And, above all, if you can do all that, then you can and *should* accomplish damn near anything.

This is about keeping ***your* faith in *yourself.***

Help Yourself Reminders

- IN LIFE, PAIN IS TEMPORARY, WHILE THE RE-SULTS OF QUITTING ON ONESELF LAST FOR-EVER!

- NO MATTER HOW DIFFICULT THINGS MAY AP-PEAR, MAINTAIN THE MIND-SET THAT *YOU* WILL AND MUST SUCCEED.

- IF YOU'VE ALREADY SURVIVED THE "HARD STUFF" AT THIS STAGE IN YOUR LIFE, THEN YOU DAMN WELL SHOULD BE ABLE TO ACCOMPLISH ANYTHING.

- ON THE ROAD OF LIFE YOU HAVE NO IDEA WHAT YOU'RE MADE OF UNTIL YOU PUSH YOURSELF BEYOND THE NORM.

- NO MATTER WHAT, KEEP *YOUR* FAITH IN *YOU*.

Chapter 10

Always an Option

Keep this in your back pocket: While a fair amount of folks do commit, a majority of them through ignorance or even arrogance "overreach" whatever it is they commit to in the first place. By this I mean that some folks, who may have the most sincere intentions at the time they make their pledge, set such outrageous goals for themselves, with little chance of their achieving "whatever" no matter how much they pour themselves into their goal. *Then* they may find themselves in a worse position than before, thus making them extremely reluctant to stand up and commit to other situations in the future.

Let's say you've been putting off studying for that big exam the last two weeks. Now, the night prior, push comes to shove, and you've finally "committed." You're going to cram in more than three hundred pages of text and a mountain-sized amount of notes. Good for you. Impossible? No. Realistic? Duh, what do you think? (On average there is anywhere from two hundred to four hundred words per page, taking an average of three to five minutes per page. That's reading, not comprehending, which takes longer. You had better drink a lot of coffee, for it will take you around twelve to fifteen hours of nonstop reading. And, again, that's without that pile of notes to sort through. On second thought, I'd forgo the coffee. You won't have time to pee.) Even as you read those pages and notes, your focus will be on how much more you have left to cover rather than on truly understanding the material.

The same thing applies if you're late for school or work. You overslept, didn't manage your time, had a problem that diverted your attention, got into an argument with so-and-so, whatever. You're now "committed" to get to where you're going, but your focus is just getting there by shaving every second possible instead of driving safely. And because you've only been driving for five years or less, you are still relatively new to this skill, and statistics show that if you don't get into an accident injuring yourself or more likely someone else, you'll probably be in the 75 percent category in which 75 percent of all speeding tickets are issued when the driver is fighting to make up for being two minutes late—a mere 120 seconds late.

It's an equal set of principles when it comes to your finances with the "splurge now and make teeny, tiny, minimal payments later," which in fact you could be making for many, many years to make up for the one incident of binge shopping. There is also the seriousness if not deadly effects of "tinkering" with your body by stupidly doing whatever one thinks is necessary just to slip into a smaller dress size or the vain hope of looking like one of those models you see in glorified magazines who shock their system through dangerous if not deadly yo-yo dieting or God knows whatever else. Even though those models represent not even 1 percent of the nearly 7 billion folks who, like you and your friends, live in a real world without the aid of computerized photo enhancement.

Am I making myself clear here?

Please understand I'm in no way trying to confuse you or throw cold water on whatever goals and pledges you've made. However, over the years I've seen so many adults, especially the "couch potatoes," who exclaim with all the bravado they can muster that *they* are suddenly going to conquer Mount Everest when they can't even get up to change the TV channel, let alone summit a small hill.

Baby Steps

Yes, I want you to commit and do so with all your heart. But at least for now, so as not to set yourself up for a possible fiasco and any disappointment that follows, I want you to develop a solid foundation, to focus on things that are just beyond your reach but are in fact obtainable.

So when it comes to studying, don't try to cram in X amount of pages overnight but, rather, prepare just a tad bit more every day than you normally would. *This way* the pressure won't build up inside you, and you can be more relaxed and allow your mind to absorb more material. Ta-da!

If you'll allow me, here's what you do. If you follow this procedure, I promise your scores will improve. 1) Prepare. The day you know your test date, and when you return home, tidy up your room. Studies show that putting your study area in order helps makes a person more relaxed and in control of his or her setting. 2) Eat a light snack—nothing too heavy so it doesn't make you sleepy afterward. Fruit is preferable. Stay away from junk foods or those sugar-filled sodas so you don't "crash" from that "sugar high" later. 3) Freshen up. Clean off any grit or sweat from your day, and if it makes you feel more comfortable, change into loose clothing. As a side note, music is fine but only as background noise that doesn't draw your attention from your studies. No matter your taste—pop, rock, rap, jazz, whatever—I recommend anything that has a subtle beat.

Now you are ready to attack your work! Let's say it's Monday. Well, all I want you to do is study an extra five minutes that day. That's it. But, when I say *study,* I mean no interruptions, no daydreaming, no goofing around, no yakking on the phone, no looking at your fingernails. Focus all your attention on your task. Five extra minutes, that's all. And when you think about it, it's not all that much. A set of TV commercials runs longer than that.

This is something you can easily do.

Another thing about that five extra minutes: I want you to study out loud. Why? Because not only does this automatically force you to concentrate more, but the brain has a way of recalling what it hears. Also, when you're talking out loud, speak slowly and clearly, *and* try to break down whatever you're studying into some sort of rhyme, maybe something like "In 1492, Columbus sailed the ocean *blue.*" Just as when you were a preschool child reciting your ABCs, these rhymes not only make you more relaxed but help provide a reference in case you become frustrated or tangled up when taking your actual test.

On Tuesday, repeat everything—prep, eat, and relax—

but now study an extra ten minutes. Then on Wednesday, study an extra fifteen. Now on Thursday, the day before the big test, I want you to study for . . . unless it's absolutely necessary: zero extra minutes. That's right, zero extra minutes. Why? I want you to reduce any pressure, chill out, and get a good night's sleep. Then on test day I want you to walk in as if you're about to take the field at a sporting event, with your chin held high and the confidence of the outcome of the test. From now on I don't want your philosophy to be "I'm going to blow it" but, instead, again just as in any sporting match, "I'm gonna kick some butt."

Commitment, *yes!* But with small consistent steps that you can achieve.

If you wish to get into a smaller dress size, which may depend on a multitude of things, I'd suggest a formula of deleting all those sodas and replacing them with water. Maybe add a little more walking to your daily routine.

When it comes to finances, whenever I ask adults, "Who wants to be a millionaire?" particularly those in the corporate world, every hand shoots up. "All right," I tease, "here's what you do. If you want to get rich, if you want to be rolling in it, all you need to do is save money!" That's it. Save more than you spend as early in life as possible. Save, save, save, save. If you get an allowance, stash half of it away. If you're working, when you get that next raise, put half of it into a long-term savings account. Now I understand as you're reading this you might try to justify to yourself: "I can't do that. I've got all the time in the world. I, ah, need . . . I gotta get that thing I've wanted . . . ." But hold on a second and sincerely ask yourself: "When it comes to spending, is it a matter of need or a matter of want? Is it something you truly desire or just another 'thing' you crave right now?"

Keep It Simple

With all these types of examples and other elements that are vital in your life, it's basically a matter of establishing an easy, realistic, obtainable approach coupled with the day-in, day-out pledge to carry it out. It's basically that simple.

As I've stated before, I truly don't care all that much if you get straight A's, are a certain body size, or become a part of the lifestyles of the rich and the famous. I *am* concerned about your making that commitment to enhance and enrich your life.

The bottom line: No matter what, **you forge ahead.** Even in the worst of situations **you** come up with a plan, any plan, and I expect **you** to see it through. Just keep using **your** head, and I promise that sooner or later **you** will break through.

Forced to Commit

For me it was the decision or *option* in the beginning of consciously or subconsciously forging ahead that propelled me through the most degrading and loneliest times of my life. As a child there were times, when Mother was "done" with me, that she would literally throw me down the stairs of the basement. Of all the physical torture, feeling subhuman was the worst. After crying and replaying what had happened, I'd collect myself. One time, scared and alone, the shivering pain seemed more than I could bear. Without thinking or analyzing as I normally did, I started counting backward from sixty. When I reached zero, I took a deep breath and reevaluated my situation. Feeling just a little bit better, I counted another sixty seconds. That day I must have counted down for more than a half hour, and with each minute the pain, coupled with the humiliating feeling inside me, subsided. That one diversion not only took my mind off my latest situation but gave me a sense of control and self-worth and, more important, elevated my life in a totally different direction.

Sometime later Mother developed a "game" of filling the bathtub with cold water and having me lie in it for hours. Rather than concentrating on the temperature of the liquid and how humiliated I felt lying in the tub completely exposed, I reapplied the technique that had worked for me in the basement. Stretched out naked in the tub there were only two things I could do: focus on how cold the water was or concentrate on anything but the temperature of the water. (Get it?) Again, it didn't change my actual situation, but as I've demonstrated before, at the time it was enough to get me through.

I became committed to keeping my vow and would grab on to any shred of hope, *anything,* no matter how minuscule, desperate, or degrading, in order to prevail. To endure all that I had just to end up quitting on myself was *not* an option. After being burned on the arm, I felt things would probably go from bad to worse. I also knew that no matter how much I tried to mentally disconnect myself from the day-to-day situations with my mother while trying to focus on remaining strong on the inside, none of it could change my physical environment. (Remember,

90 percent of all problems are in your head.) All I had to do was develop simple ideas to remain alive.

Immediately after the incident with my burnt arm, I began to look at my predicament differently. Rather than waste time and energy crying all the time in the base-ment, I started to apply those precious hours alone to come up with plans on how to react to my next encounter with Mother.

For years I had been trained that whenever Mother walked down the main hallway, no matter whether I was performing a chore such as picking up debris from the carpet with my fingers, I was required to instantly spring up and stand against the wall in the position of address. But whenever I did, I just could not seem to stop my body from shaking. Mother, feeding off my fear, would take joy in hitting me until I fell back down.

So I came up with a plan that would begin by shaving a second or two before I sprang up (a proven idea that I improved upon after the gas stove incident). Then I'd dip my head slightly to the right while tightening the muscles of my arms, chest, and neck.

Alone with all that time on my hands, I'd recall how Mother never missed an opportunity to strike me, and when she did, it was usually with her right hand, which landed on the left side of my chest. So, by exposing and tightening that area of my body and knowing what was coming, it really didn't hurt all that much even though I would still crumble to the floor, fulfilling "Her" pleasure of humiliating me.

It is the same mentality when you're playing sports— baseball, for example. You really have to think ahead about how to execute a possible play with every pitch thrown and every swing of the bat. Let's say there is a ground ball coming at your area in the outfield. Now you can do nothing, blow the play by freezing up while brainwashing yourself with "I can't get it. I'll never get there in time. I'm gonna blow it." Or you can stay ahead of the game and with a little raw determination sprint over, scoop up the ball, and make the important cutoff play. You may not discover until later that your pants got torn and you skinned your knee while making the play. Are you hurt? Not in the slightest. What truly stands out is that because of your focus and determination you came up with a simple plan and followed it through. The skinned knee was the tiny price you paid for internal accomplishment.

One of the most important things I've learned is that when it comes to problems, especially extremely critical situations, most of them can be solved not with far-out, high-tech wizardry but with simple, off-the-cuff, commonsense deeds of action. Period. For the most part, lots of folks spend more time looking for some elaborate answer with no real intention of unraveling their problem rather than implementing a solution that's right in front of them.

Example: Mother decides not to feed me. Solution: I feed myself. Truth be told, I stole food, which of course was absolutely wrong. Yet as I sat on my hands or stood leaning against a wooden beam in the basement, with no sustenance for days as a form of punishment, while trying to capture sounds and scents of a family dining upstairs, I became desperate. In my quest to sustain myself, I came up with hundreds—and I do mean *hundreds*—of plans. And while I developed and then dissected over-the-top elaborate schemes—how fast I would have to run to a local store at lunchtime in order to snatch a certain item of food in a certain aisle without getting caught, only to end up having Mother bust me when I tried to smuggle my prize into her house—it was actually the small, simple possibilities I employed that put food in my belly.

Acting as Mother's servant when clearing the table and washing the dinner dishes, I'd scrape the leftover food from the plates into my mouth or my pocket for later. When caught and then punished, I'd carefully sneak weeks-old food from the back of the refrigerator. When that plan was foiled, I took food from Mother's pantry. When that idea no longer worked, I'd burrow through to the bottom of the large downstairs garbage can, until Mother countered my ploy by pouring ammonia or bleach in the metal receptacle.

It didn't matter to me how nauseating or despicable my actions were. I had no one but myself to rely on. I made a commitment, and knowing the outcome, I only had myself to see it through.

When I knew the house became "locked up," was I out of options? No. I simply set my sights where there was lots of food with lots of alternatives: school. I began by taking sandwiches from the lunch boxes in the hallway before the beginning of class. I'd stroll over and bend down, acting as if I were tying my shoes. But I only stole half, for I didn't want anyone else to go hungry. After a short while, because of the numerous sudden complaints, the teachers would take the lunch boxes and brown paper bags and lock them in their classroom closets.

When that option expired, I'd sneak into the cafeteria to snatch all the tater tots and hot dogs my hands could carry—until the staff discovered another unexpected rash of missing food, forcing them to lock that room until lunchtime.

Again, I confess I felt humiliated beyond words. At times when I couldn't scrounge any food, I became extremely upset, especially when everyone else at school stuffed their faces with an abundance of treats and not even finishing their lunches before carelessly tossing the remains into a garbage can right in front of me as if I were invisible. *Those* kids—who wore *real* clothes, clean clothes without holes, who slept in real beds with warm blankets and not on some moldy army cot with moldy smelly rags that I'd use to wrap around my feet—*those* kids had everything while *poor little ol' me* had . . .

Allow me, if you will, to go on a slight riff. Don't waste your time and dilute your focus by stupidly believing "the grass is always greener on the other side." By that I mean those who constantly whine, "So-and-so has more," "Life isn't fair," "They have a new car," "So-and-so has her own DVD player," "What about me?" "I want, I want, I want!"

What about you? What is it that you intend to do about your plight? Again, if there's something you want, you will find a way to make it a reality. Want tickets to that concert? Buy them yourself. Don't have the money? Save up. Don't have an allowance? Get a job. Have a job? Put in more hours. In other words, do something about it. **You** do something about it. Don't look for Mom, Dad, your cute grandma, your teachers, or anyone else. Do what you have to do to make it happen.

The reality is that sooner or later everybody learns (or should have learned) that they and they alone must become self-reliant. The day I became filled with rage about how everyone else had more and how unfair life could be *did not* help me at all. If anything, it sucked away my time and energy, and, most important, it diverted me from my focus. Again, it's good to get things out, to purge everything from your system, but don't allow it to dominate you or deflect you from what you're striving to achieve. *That* tendency could cripple you.

Sometimes the Answer Is Right in Front of You

One lunch period, with my shoulders slumped over in despair, my ears picked up the distinctive sound of something hitting the inside of a metal garbage can. "Garbage can" my brain yelled out. Lunchtime meant food. Leftover food gets tossed in the can, which means—just as I had at Mother's house—I could rummage through the receptacle and feed myself!

Suddenly any cold thoughts of jealousy that began to brew evaporated. I again fixated on coming up with a simple plan. Since there were four garbage cans in the school yard, I figured I had four options to feed myself. In a matter of days I quickly learned that if I snuck over to retrieve anything possible from the first garbage can, the janitor had already emptied it. So where do you think I ran to next? Not garbage can number two but number three. Why? By the time I'd get to the second garbage can, it, too, would be emptied as well as the third and fourth can.

I made that mistake once. I screwed up, I learned, I adapted, and I moved on.

My point is: Even when you have a plan and when

things don't go as you hoped, I want you to—*I expect you* to—immediately, just as you would in sports, come up with another alternative and, if necessary, another and another and another. Just don't quit on yourself.

Keep plugging away. Day by day. Step by step. Just like Erik who got to the summit of mighty Mount Everest with no vision, be careful where and how you proceed with every foot placed in front of you. When you slip and fall, although you know that one slight mistake may take away your golden dream, like Michelle Kwan brush yourself off and continue your routine. And like Lance Armstrong, make *every* second count.

This simple mentality helped keep me alive for the next four years, until the day I was rescued. Of course not all my ideas panned out. If anything, they probably failed half the time, and then, of course, Mother would unleash her fury on me. But after licking my wounds I had the satisfaction that at least I tried. But I always strived to never cave in. And during the hard times when I had nothing left, I—like *billions* of folks—somehow found a way to muster through. My commitment gave me a certain pride I would never have experienced had it not been for my situation. And half of those failures were better than doing nothing. I was at least dealing with my mother.

It was never about defeating "Her" or showing "Her" she couldn't break me as much as it was simply my learning to rely on myself by striving forward by any means possible.

But you cannot and will not move on with your life if you do not commit, truly commit to yourself in some sense. Whether it's letting go of a past issue, trying to dig yourself out of a current situation, or improving your odds of success, any declaration you make without constant, achievable follow-through is a hollow pledge. A hollow commitment is destined to failure. And you deserve better, much better than that.

Therefore, commit to a plan. Keep it simple. Adapt when needed. And implement necessary changes on a regular basis.

You just never know. The answer to your situation could be right in front of you, in the most unlikely place. That symbolic "garbage can" just might contain a vast amount of treasures that you've been searching for. All you have to do is be willing to simply reach in and grab your prize.

Help Yourself Reminders

- DEVELOP SMALL YET OBTAINABLE GOALS THAT YOU CAN EASILY ADJUST AND IMPLEMENT ON A DAILY BASIS.

- WHATEVER YOUR OBJECTIVE, KEEP IN MIND THAT THE SIMPLER THE PLAN, THE EASIER IT IS TO FULFILL.

- SOMETIMES A PROBLEM CAN WORK IN YOUR FAVOR BY FORCING YOU TO COMMIT TO RE-SOLVE THAT ISSUE AS WELL AS OTHERS IN THE FUTURE.

- GATHER YOUR FACTS, SEEK COUNSEL IF NEEDED, BUT LEARN TO DEPEND ON YOURSELF.

- REMEMBER, YOU ARE YOUR BEST OPTION TO TAKE A STAND AND MAKE A DIFFERENCE IN YOUR LIFE.

A FINAL WORD

With all my heart I hope you discovered some things about yourself and are now able to apply them as building blocks to enhance your life.

In Part One we spent a lot of time dealing with your life, about coming to terms with a negative past, acknowledging certain apprehensions, and maintaining your internal focus to keep you on track.

Part Two dealt with the choices you make, that no matter what the situation or the number of excuses, decisions rest with you and you alone. That you can allow your problems to accumulate and dominate you, or you can purge them from your life and be done with all that needless junk once and for all. And, finally, hate is a cancer that **will** destroy anything it attaches itself to, so in order to move on, you need to free yourself by learning to forgive.

In Part Three, the final section, we went into the power of your commitment, that if you can survive all that you have thus far, then at this age and phase of your life you can in fact overcome just about anything else that life may throw your way. You can set small yet achievable goals. That your solution most likely stands in front of you, and you and you alone are the person who has to see things through in order to achieve your personal desires.

Now you may have noticed that Part One was rather long. This was deliberate. I wanted to lay a solid foundation for you. I firmly believe you cannot achieve a certain level or status in life unless you first deal with the situations from your past. Part Two had a little less material that built on the premise of your responsibility until you reached the summit of the book by dealing with the capability of resolve, which in fact makes you the independent person you've most likely wanted to be all along.

Think of the sections as a pyramid. You need each and every level to help you get to the top of your threshold of your final independence.

So now, whenever problems creep up on you, as problems will, or when you feel you've fallen a few levels, just go back to that particular section in the book, review it, underline it, write it on a three-by-five card or your computer, and keep it with you. Apply the material until you feel you're back on top again.

But remember that this book, or any other resource for that matter, is not the end-all cure for everything. As long as you're living, you will be adjusting and learning, going backward and forward on a multitude of issues. The truth is, you're never going to get everything just right. Life is never going to be perfect. But these tools you've acquired thus far will definitely help you in your journey!

And now that we've come to the end, here are a few more words. First, I'm very proud of you! You finished what you've set out to do. It takes a certain person of maturity to stop and take a deep look into themselves. So give yourself some credit that you took on a challenging task and saw it through.

Remember: No matter what the future holds, **you are a person of value.** So hold your head up and carry yourself with pride.

Take care of yourself. Work hard, sacrifice, and forge ahead, yes, but enjoy the wonder and splendor of the adventure along the way.

Take lots of photos. Trust me, in a short amount of time you'll wake up one day and discover just how fleeting time can be, so take lots of colorful memories with you. Snap pictures not only of the great times but a few when things aren't going so good. Why? Good times as well as bad times are part of your lifetime; they combine to give you that quiet sense of appreciation when you have overcome all that you have during the course of your entire life. So when you've reached that summit, when you've conquered against all odds, you won't forget how you got there.

Keep moving forward. Keep learning. Go "out there." Do things. Explore your world and all it entails. Step outside yourself. Don't be too afraid to take a chance or two.

Don't be too concerned about wanting to grow up too fast. Enjoy the time and the opportunities you have now. Laugh. Laugh a lot.

And, finally, the **big one:** No matter what happens in the course of your life, I beg of you, don't forget your dreams. Don't settle just to settle. Don't give your best away. Don't cheat yourself of your greatness. Don't forget your passion, the deep desires you've carried within you since you were knee-high.

So now go out there and live that adventure. Have fun. And have fun *now!*

And if you ever feel alone or feel that just can't carry on, just look to those who truly care for you. And if they're not around, well, crack open this book, and I'll be right beside you, rooting for you . . . to better yourself.

Good luck, my friend. Stay strong and stay focused.

God's blessings to you!

—Dave Pelzer

GLOSSARY

Accumulate   transitive verb. To collect.
   Synonyms: gather, stockpile

Adamant   adjective. To be stern and persistent.
   Synonyms: stubborn, uncompromising

Adversity   noun. In a troubled state.
   Synonyms: misfortune, hardship

Affliction   noun. A cause of suffering and pain.
   Synonyms: pain, loss

Analyze   transitive verb. To examine something in detail.
   Synonyms: break down, evaluate

Anarchy   noun. The absence of governmental authority.
   Synonyms: chaos, disorder

Animosity   noun. An intense feeling of hostility.
   Synonyms: hatred, bad blood

Annihilate   transitive verb. To destroy completely.
   Synonyms: ruin, demolish

Appease transitive verb. To satisfy by giving in to the demands of someone.
Synonyms: to please, gratify

Arduous adjective. Something that is difficult to do.
Synonyms: backbreaking, hard

Articulation noun. The act of speaking clearly.
Synonyms: speech, expressing oneself

Asinine adjective. Something that is stupid or foolish.
Synonyms: silly, moronic

Asphyxiate transitive verb. To become unconscious from lack of oxygen to the brain.
Synonyms: suffocate, stifle

Atrocities plural noun. Cruel and offensive acts.
Synonyms: wickedness, evil

Barrio noun. Spanish word meaning neighborhood.
Synonyms: territory, community

Bravado noun. False confidence and courage.
Synonyms: boasting, arrogance

Camelot noun. The legend of King Arthur and his court at Camelot; i.e., a legendary paradise.

Carcass noun. A dead body.
Synonyms: empty shell, dead animal

Circumstances plural noun. A situation affecting a person.
Synonyms: event, condition

Clarity   noun. The quality of being clear.
   Synonyms: definition, understandable

Competent   adjective. Having the capability.
   Synonyms: able, prepared

Complacent   adjective. Lack of emotion.
   Synonyms: content, apathy

Consciously   adverb. To have an awareness of one's
   thoughts.
   Synonyms: deliberately, willfully

Cranium   noun. The part of the skull that contains the
   brain.

Crevasse   noun. A deep crack.
   Synonyms: gorge, ravine

Cusp   noun. A time of transition.
   Synonyms: intersection, projection

Debris   noun. Broken pieces of something.
   Synonyms: rubble, scattered remains

Deceit   noun. A dishonest action.
   Synonyms: lie, trickery

Decipher   transitive verb. Make out the meaning of
   something.
   Synonyms: explain, interpret

Deficiency   noun. Lacking in something.
   Synonyms: incomplete, unfinished

Delusional   adjective. Irrationally or falsely believing.
  Synonyms: deceptive, misleading

Demeanor   noun. One's outward behavior.
  Synonyms: conduct, attitude

Despicable   adjective. Deserving of scorn.
  Synonyms: mean, detestable

Deviant   adjective. Contrasting with what is natural or normal.
  Synonyms: twisted, unnatural

Expletive   noun. An exclamation.
  Synonyms: curse, a nonsense word

Fiasco   noun. A complete and utter failure.
  Synonyms: mess, botch

Fidget   intransitive verb. To move nervously.
  Synonyms: squirm, wriggle

Forgo   transitive verb. To do without.
  Synonyms: abstain, give up

Fringe   noun. An outer edge.
  Synonyms: border, outskirts

Glutton   noun. One with an unhealthy indulgence for something.
  Synonyms: greed, overeater, pig

Gnaw   verb. Consume bit by bit.
  Synonyms: worry, pester

Guttural   adjective. Harsh vocal sounds.
  Synonyms: raspy, throaty

Hindrance   noun. An obstacle.
   Synonyms: prevention, limitation, impediment

Imperative   adjective. Something that is urgent.
   Synonyms: pressing, necessary

Incense   transitive verb. To make very angry.
   Synonyms: to infuriate, to enrage, to arouse

Indomitable   adjective. Not easily defeated.
   Synonyms: unstoppable, determined

Inebriated   adjective. Intoxicated.
   Synonyms: drunk, loaded

Inevitable   adjective. Something that is certain to happen.
   Synonyms: unavoidable, destined

Inferior   adjective. To be lower in status.
   Synonyms: second-class, lesser

Ingrain   transitive verb. To fix in one's mind.
   Synonyms: deep-rooted, fixed

Lackadaisical   adjective. Showing a lack of interest.
   Synonyms: unenthusiastic, lazy

Mantra   noun. A chant that aids in meditation.
   Synonyms: hymn, psalm

Mediocre   adjective. Something that is barely acceptable.
   Synonyms: average, ordinary

Megalomania   noun. A mental disorder characterized by a delusion of power.
   Synonyms: crazy, lunatic

Mesmerize   transitive verb. To cause to be spellbound.
   Synonyms: hypnotize, fascinate

Meticulous   adjective. Paying close attention to detail.
   Synonyms: precise, exact

Minuscule   adjective. Very small.
   Synonyms: tiny, mini

Minute   adjective. An exact detail.
   Synonyms: least, slight

Mire   intransitive verb. To become stuck in a difficult situation.
   Synonyms: entangled, involved

Narcissistic   adjective. Excessive interest in one's self.
   Synonyms: vain, self-important

Naught   noun. For nothing.
   Synonyms: zero, nil

Nonchalant   adjective. To be indifferent to something.
   Synonyms: detached, unexcited

Obscene   adjective. Contrary to accepted morality.
   Synonyms: repulsive, vulgar

Optimistic   adjective. To take the most hopeful view of matters.
   Synonyms: positive, hopeful

Pathetic   adjective. Deserving of pity and sorrow.
   Synonyms: sad, tragic

Pediatrician   noun. A medical doctor who deals with the care of infants and children.

Perpetrator   noun. Someone who does something evil or criminal.
Synonyms: evildoer, criminal

Perseverance   noun. The continuing of a course of action in spite of difficulty.
Synonyms: persistence, determination

Pertinent   adjective. To be relevant to a situation.
Synonyms: fitting, appropriate

Phenomenal   adjective. An extraordinary situation or person.
Synonyms: sensational, exceptional

Pivotal   adjective. A person or thing on which something depends.
Synonyms: central, critical

Placid   adjective. Calm.
Synonyms: quiet, peacefulness

Porcelain   noun. Hard white variety of ceramic ware.

Predicament   noun. An unpleasant situation.
Synonyms: dilemma, quandary

Prejudice   noun. Preconceived intolerance or hatred.
Synonyms: unfairness, bias

Proactive   adjective. Taking control of a situation by causing something to happen before it happens.
Synonyms: taking charge, hands-on

Procrastinating transitive verb. To put off doing something until later.
Synonyms: delaying, hesitating

Pronunciation noun. The sound of a spoken word.
Synonyms: speech pattern, manner of speaking

Provocation noun. Act of inciting; to stir things up.
Synonyms: reason, stimulus

Psyche noun. Subconscious mind.
Synonyms: soul, mind

Psychological adjective. Of the mind or emotions.

Reclusive adjective. Living a secluded life.
Synonyms: isolated, lone

Regurgitate intransitive verb. To bring back up partially digested food.
Synonyms: throw up, vomit

Reign intransitive verb. A period of rule or dominance; hold sway.
Synonyms: obtain, "call the shots" (slang)

Repercussion noun. An indirect reaction to some event.
Synonyms: reaction, consequence

Resilience noun. Capability of recovering strength and spirit.
Synonyms: rebound, flexibility

Retribution noun. Punishment for the evil one has done.
Synonyms: vengeance, justice

Ruse   noun. A ploy.
    Synonyms: trick, deception

Sadistic   adjective. Getting pleasure out of mistreating
    others.
    Synonyms: cruel, ruthless

Sanctuary   noun. A place of protection.
    Synonyms: refuge, retreat

Solace   noun. To take comfort from grief.
    Synonyms: relief, support

Sustenance   noun. Means of nourishment.
    Synonyms: food, rations

Tenacity   noun. To hold firmly to an idea.
    Synonyms: stubbornness, persistence

Tormentor   noun. One who causes great pain and
    mental anguish.
    Synonyms: mistreat, torturer

Vengeance   noun. Punishment inflicted in retaliation.
    Synonyms: retribution, revenge

Venture   noun. Something that involves risk.
    Synonyms: chance, gamble

Verbiage   noun. A manner of expressing words.
    Synonyms: wordiness, talk

Vernacular   adjective. Common everyday language.
    Synonyms: simple, language, native, local

ACKNOWLEDGMENTS

I wish to thank agent provocateur Ms. Laurie Liss. Laurie, throughout the years, with our endless talks and strategies of how to create an aspiring new tome and all that time together in faraway places, I've realized how much you care not only about every book of every client, but also about truly making a difference in the lives of others.

A big thank-you to Mrs. Gabrielle Norwood for taking over the helm as executive director of the office at D-Esprit, which at times can make the television series *West Wing* and action hero Jack Bauer of Fox's *24* fame look like they're in a coma. For as long as God allows, the frenzy, chaos, drama, and adventure will continue. I'm proud of you!

A huge thank-you to Mr. Rey Thayne for all your time, patience, and humble dedication, which never go unnoticed. I also wish to thank you for doing all you can to keep me on track, and staying ahead of me so as to make my life all the easier. But mostly, thanks, Rey, for your trust and being a good friend. Bless you, *Sir*.

A special thank-you to Mrs. Carole Baron of Dutton. Thanks for sticking up for the rights of the small guy in the business and being a lady of character and grace. It was an honor to serve under you. I will miss you, "Auntie Carole."

To Mr. Brian Tart, president and publisher of Dutton, for your time, guidance, and for giving me a wide berth when it comes to the written word. But mainly for always permitting me to go a little bit more and more "out there" as a writer with a cause.

A special thank-you to Ms. Jean Ann Rose of Dutton's public relations department, for all your time, absolute dedication, and the hours of humor when I had been up for days without end during my *La Tour La Farce* that weird January of 2004. You're a bug!

A heartfelt benediction to Marsha Pelzer of First Class Publishing Projects. All those years together and all the sacrifices that were made that the world will never know. Whether working together or as husband and wife, we gave all that we had. In the end, at least we can step back and truly state without reservation, *we* did our damnedest in helping others in dire need. Even now . . . not a day goes by . . . *In Her Family.*

Lastly, to Dr. Hunter S. Thompson, a mighty dinosaur whose outlandish, unprecedented vernacular and stinging wit will be missed by a world that has become far too dark, serious, and twisted. Thanks for everything, Doc!

KEYNOTES

Dave is a living testament of resilience, faith in humanity, and personal responsibility. Dave's unique and inspirational outlook on life, coupled with his Robin Williams–like wit and sense of humor, entertains and encourages business professionals with real-life information to overcome obstacles while living life to its fullest. This is what has made Dave one of the most exceptional and unequaled personalities in the public-speaking arena today.

Dave also continues to provide specific programs to those who work in the human services and educational fields.

For additional information on having Dave speak to your group, please write, call, fax, or visit our Web site at:

D-Esprit
P.O. Box 1846
Rancho Mirage, CA 92270
Phone: 760-321-4452
Fax: 760-321-6842
www.DavePelzer.com

And for those who wish to write, please keep in mind that due to the large volume of letters we receive daily, as much as we try, we will not be able to answer every letter. But we sincerely thank you for taking your valuable time to write us. God bless.

—*Dave Pelzer*

ABOUT THE AUTHOR

A former air force aircrew member, Dave proudly served in the United States Air Force for more than thirteen years. He played a major role in Operations Just Cause, Desert Shield, and Desert Storm. Dave was selected for the unique task of midair refueling of the once highly secretive SR-71 Blackbird and the F-117 Stealth Fighter. While serving in the air force, Dave worked in juvenile hall and other programs involving "youth-at-risk" throughout California.

Dave's exceptional accomplishments include commendations from Presidents Reagan, Bush, Clinton, and George W. Bush, as well as other various heads of state. While maintaining an international active-duty flight schedule, Dave was the recipient of the 1990 JCPenney Golden Rule Award, making him the California Volunteer of the Year. In 1993, Dave was honored as one of the Ten Outstanding Young Americans (TOYA), joining a distinguished group of alumni that includes Chuck Yeager, Christopher Reeve, Anne Bancroft, John F. Kennedy, Orson Welles, and Walt Disney. In 1994, Dave was the *only* American to be selected as one of The Outstanding Young Persons of the World (TOYP) for his efforts involving child-abuse awareness and prevention, as well as for promoting resilience and self-responsibility in others. During the centennial Olympic Games, Dave was a torchbearer, carrying the coveted flame.

Dave is the author of six other inspirational books including: *A Child Called "It,"* which has been on the *New York Times* bestseller list for more than six years; *A Man Named Dave,* a bestseller for more than a year and a half; *Help Yourself,* which was also an instant *New York Times* bestseller; and his coming-of-age timepiece, *The Privilege of Youth*. Dave's books have been on the bestseller list for more than thirteen years combined.

Dave is currently at work on his next book, which deals with leadership values for the everyday person, titled *Your Resolve*.

When not on the road or with his son, Stephen, Dave lives a quiet life in Southern California with his box turtle named Chuck.

For more information you can visit Dave's Web site at www.DavePelzer.com.

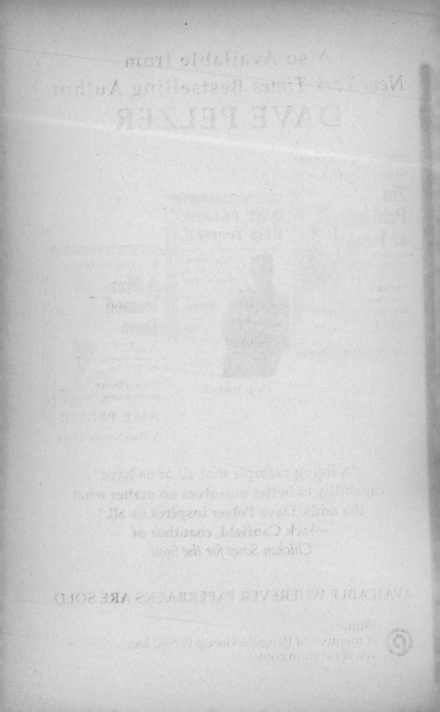

Also Available from
New York Times Bestselling Author
DAVE PELZER

The Privilege of Youth

Help Yourself

A Man Named Dave